Legal Self-Help Guide

Estate Planning

In

Plain-English

Legal Self-Help Guide

Estate Planning

In

Plain-English

Sanket Mistry, JD, MIA, edited by J.T. Levine, JD, MFA

ISBN 13: 978-1-940788-10-4
ISBN 10: 1-940788-10-2

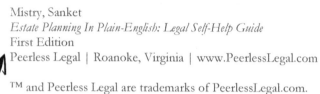

Mistry, Sanket
Estate Planning In Plain-English: Legal Self-Help Guide
First Edition
Peerless Legal | Roanoke, Virginia | www.PeerlessLegal.com

™ and Peerless Legal are trademarks of PeerlessLegal.com.

Peerless Legal books are available for special promotions. For details, contact Peerless Legal by email at sales@peerlesslegal.com, or visit www.PeerlessLegal.com.

While the author has made every effort to provide accurate telephone numbers and internet addresses at the time of publication, neither the publisher nor author assume any responsibility for errors or changes that occur after publication. The publisher does not have any control over, and does not assume any responsibility for, author or third-party websites or their content.

This publication is designed to provide accurate and authoritative information in regard to the subject matters covered. It is sold with the understanding that the publisher and author are not engaged in rendering legal, accounting, or other professional services. If legal advice or other expert assistance is required, the services of a competent professional should be sought.

From a *Declaration of Principles jointly adopted by a Committee of the American Bar Association and a Committee of Publishers*
THIS PRODUCT IS NOT A SUBSITUTE FOR LEGAL ADVICE.
Disclaimer required by Texas statutes.

DISCLAIMER

Laws change constantly. Every effort has been made to provide the most up-to-date information. However, the author, publisher, and any and all persons or entities involved in any way in the preparation, publication, sale, or distribution of this publication disclaim any and all representations or warranties, express or implied, about the outcome or methods of use of this publication, and assume no liability for claims, losses, or damages arising from the use or misuse of this publication. All responsibilities for legal effects or consequences of any document prepared from, or action taken in reliance upon information contained in this publication are disclaimed. The reader should not rely on this author or this publisher for professional advice. Users of this publication intending to use this publication for preparation of legal documents are advised to check specifically on the current, applicable laws in any jurisdiction in which they intend the documents to be effective. Make sure you are using the most recent edition.

Is This Legal Self-Help Guide for You?

The Peerless Legal mission is to empower individuals by giving them legal self-help tools. The Legal Self-Help Guide series was created as the embodiment of that mission.

The goal of this Guide is to provide you with the information you need to understand your legal rights and responsibilities. In doing so, we hope you will be able to resolve your legal issues yourself or know enough to feel confident in your decision to hire a licensed attorney. This Guide provides a meaningful alternative to most of the books in law libraries. Peerless Legal's goal is for you to be able to understand this material.

You are not alone in choosing self-help. Everyone faces legal issues at some point in their life. While most of us have the capacity to understand our legal rights and responsibilities, finding good legal information can be daunting. As the costs associated with legal representation rise, more and more people are opting to take certain legal matters into their own hands.

In this Guide, Peerless Legal provides you with meaningful alternatives to costly legal representation for legal issues you can handle yourself. This Guide is a plain-English alternative to the legal jargon that fills most legal books.

This book is for you if:

- you want to handle your own legal issues,
- you are not sure whether the legal issue you are facing merits the high cost of an attorney,
- you are in the process of looking for competent, legal representation, but are unsure how to evaluate legal services,

- you have retained an attorney and are unsure whether your attorney is competently handling your legal issues,
- or you want to know more about a specific legal topic.

It is important to manage expectations when acting on your own behalf or with an attorney. This book's contents may differ from the requirements that are commonly used in your local jurisdiction. You can check local rules by going to the court's website, making a phone call to the office of the clerk of court, or by visiting a local law school library. Generally, law school libraries serve as Federal repositories and are open to the public during normal business hours.

Warning There are some legal issues that seem simple and straight forward, but in reality only an attorney with extensive experience on the issue would know there is an inner-tangling.**

Dedication

For my parents who taught me love and how to strive for the best, even when the best was difficult.

Acknowledgments

This book has been nothing short of a group effort. In addition to the above named dedication, I would like to thank most J.T. Levine for her gift of editing.

About the Author

Sanket Mistry earned his JD from the Walter F. George School of Law at Mercer University. He is a member of the New York State Bar and author of several books in the Legal Self-Help Guide series. He has worked, and volunteered, at a number of nonprofits, government agencies, and for-profit corporations. He also holds a BA in philosophy from Emory University and an MIA from Columbia University. He is an avid traveler and tennis player.

About the Editor

J.T. Levine earned her JD from the Walter F. George School of Law at Mercer University. She has edited several books for Peerless Legal. She is a member of the Georgia Bar. Prior to law school, she earned an MFA in Professional Writing from the Savannah College of Art and Design and a BA from the University of Miami. She is an animal lover and has a pharaoh hound named Tut.

Table of Contents

I. How to Use This Book

Get your estate in order with this book to successfully understand your legal estate documents. This book includes information about wills, powers of attorney, trusts, and other common estate planning information. It is not intended to be read as a novel. It is intended to be used as a reference guide. Pay attention to headings because they are your guide-posts. This book is laid out in a way to help you find information quickly.

This book is written in plain-English with as little legal jargon as possible. However, sometimes the legal jargon cannot be avoided. Where legal jargon is used, there is a plain-English explanation that accompanies it. If you need addition explanations, refer to the Glossary.

By the time you finish reading this book, you should be able to:

- successfully understand the uses and functions of different legal documents,
- know enough about your issue to determine whether it's complicated enough to warrant hiring an attorney, and
- understand your legal rights and responsibilities.

The book begins with a vast array of legal information that will help you create your estate documents. The information is a broad overview. Not every piece of information will pertain to you or to your jurisdiction. More information about your jurisdiction is available online at the web addresses provided in the back of this book in the Appendix.

In the beginning of the book there are detailed explanations of the important legal issues. It starts with covering the major issues relating to wills. Since many of issues also apply to powers of attorney, the powers of attorney information is included in the *Identifying Other Things to Include with Your Will* chapter. Then there is information regarding living trusts.

Next, there are additional explanations after that tell you what you should do with the legal forms after you create them.

The reminder of the book is devoted to the Appendix that includes State Specific Information, Glossary, and Index. The State Specific Information provides links to information on each of the 50 states and the District of Columbia. Laws in different states vary and you should review this section to find your specific state rules. The Glossary provides definitions to common legal terms. The Index provides cross-references.

The tools in this book will provide you with the legal information you need to help you in creating your own estate documents or to equip you with the information you need to hire a competent attorney.

II.   Wills and Powers of Attorney

1.   Introduction to Creating Your Own Will and Power of Attorney

Have you made decisions regarding what should happen to you if you are ever in a comma? Do you want to make sure that your spouse, children, or other family members are taken care of after you die? Do you want to make a will and/or power of attorney? This book can help in understanding how to do all of these things.

This book provides instructions and information to help you understand how you can create your own legal forms that can:

- control how your property will be legally disturbed when you die,
- name someone with the legal authority to follow and fulfill your wishes in your will,
- name someone to take care of your minor children,
- authorize someone to handle your finances and look after you healthcare wishes,
- name someone to manage the property you leave for your minor children,
- state your healthcare/end of life decisions,
- leave a letter to your loved ones, and
- create a living will to govern what medical procedures you want or do not want if you should become terminally ill.

The powers of attorney information is primarily in the *Identifying Other Things to Include with Your Will* chapter. Most of the information that relates to wills also applies to powers of attorney. The law does not have one set of language for wills and another set for powers of attorney. Your wills and powers of attorney should all work together.

The following chart shows the steps to create your own will. Power of attorney creation falls within "Identify Other Things." The book is also organized in this layout.

2. Basics—Functions and Uses of Wills

As you prepare to create your will the first step you need to take is to understand what a will is and why you are creating it. This chapter takes you through the basics of why you need a will and how a will can assist you in preparing to identify who will get what when you die. Along with explaining the basic functions of a will, this chapter will help you determine what you need to include in your will, and what, if any, additional resources you might need.

A. What Is a Will?

There are many kinds of wills. But, in short, a *will* is a written document that controls how your property will be disturbed when you die, who will serve as guardians of your minor children (and who will take care of the minor children's property until they reach 18), and how your property will be managed upon your death. The person whose property is affected by the will is called the *testator*. If it is your will, you are the testator.

One of the primary advantages of creating a will is that you control how your property will be distributed when you die and/or how your children will be taken care of.

Most wills created are now typed, but this is not always required. One option is to handwrite your will. A handwritten will is called a *holographic will*. A holographic will may be allowed so long as it's written entirely by your hand, signed, and dated. No witnesses are required. Not all states recognize holographic wills. Where recognized, judges, generally, disfavor them because they are often incomplete or considered unreliable documents.

An *oral will*, which is a will that is spoken, is only valid in a handful of states. Note that even where valid, there are still very specific rules. Generally, an oral will is really not a will at all.

A will that is held only electronically is called an *electronic will* and is only valid in Nevada. Although there may be a trend towards using them in the future, for now, Nevada is the only state that recognizes electronic wills. There are some added requirements for an electronic will.

Many people, including lawyers, put outdated legal jargon in a will, but it adds no extra meaning or authority to the will. Avoid such language if you don't understand it. Chances are, if you fully understand your will, then so will the judge. If you don't understand your will, then it is likely that a judge won't understand your will either. Do yourself a favor and write a will you understand.

B. Who Can Create a Will?

In general, almost anyone can create a will. The size and value of your estate is not a factor in determining if you can create a will. To legally create a valid will you need to be of:

1. legal age, and
2. "sound mind."

a) Legal Age

The legal age to create a will is usually 18, but some states have a lower age limit. For example, the lower age limit in Georgia is 14 and in Louisiana it is 16. If you are under the legal age, but in the military or married, many states allow you to create a will.

b) "Sound Mind"

A "sound mind" requires that, at the time that you *execute* the will (i.e., when you sign and date your will), you:

- know what a will is, what it does, and that you are creating a will,
- name beneficiaries that have a relationship to you that you understand, and
- you understand the nature and extent of your property.

If you meet these requirements, then the judge is not likely to ignore (set aside or disregard) your will for lack of a "sound mind." If you can understand the concept of a "sound mind," you are probably of "sound mind."

C. How to Create a Will?

The purpose of the will governs how the will is created. A will is a written document stating your wishes. The document must be signed by you, the testator, and witnessed by at least two other people (three in Vermont). The will can be changed, modified, or revoked prior to your death. The will can be probated upon your death. To be a legal will, it must go through a process known as *probate*. Probate is where the court distributes your property to the beneficiaries you name in your will or as governed by state law.

At a minimum, a will must:

1. include at least one statement giving away property or naming guardians for minor children who have no parents,
2. be signed and dated by the testator, and
3. be signed and dated by two witnesses (except in Vermont which requires three witnesses).

It is useful to also name an *executor* in your will. An executor is a person, named by you in your will, to manage your estate after you die. Some states call the executor a *personal representative*. An executor may also be referred to as an *administrator*.

D.   What Makes a Will Valid?

A will is not valid until it has been approved by probate court. In determining whether your will is valid, the court will apply the laws of the state of which you are a resident (except for real property, see next paragraph). You should create your will to be probated in the state where you are a resident. This does not mean that you have to be physically present in that state when you create your will. You can specify in your will, what your state of residence is. Generally, when a will is determined by a court to be valid in one state, then it is valid in all of the other states. If you are temporarily overseas when you create your will, your residence will be the state of your permanent residence. If are permanently overseas because you have taken on another country's citizenship or given up your U.S. citizenship then this book will not meet your needs.

When it comes to *real property*, that is real estate, the laws of the state where the property is located will govern.

E. What a Will Can Do for You

Just as there are multiple types of wills, there are multiple things a will can do, depending on your testator's relationship to your survivor's.

You can give property to individuals after you die. In doing so, you do not necessarily need to be even handed. You can give a greater share to your best friend and less to your neighbor.

You can appoint someone to handle your estate for you, called an *executor*, which is a person named by you in your will to manage your estate after you die. Some states call the executor a *personal representative* or refer to them as an *administrator*. The executor can:

- gather together all your property and distribute them according to your will,
- file paperwork for taxes or probate forms,
- hire any necessary professionals, such as attorneys or accountants,
- have the power to sell your property, and
- take other actions without having to get a court order.

A will can be used to name guardians for your minor child(ren). Naming guardians for your minor child(ren) will avoid long custody battles and allows you to have some control over who raises your minor child(ren).

If you do not want your property to be distributed immediately upon your death, you can designate in your will for the executor to create a *trust* for the child(ren) at a later date. A trust is a legal relationship where one person or entity holds legal title to, and has responsibility for, property for the financial benefit of another person or entity.

You can direct the executor to create a trust to decrease estate taxes. You can also decrease certain estate taxes by doing a more complicated estate plan. As a practical matter, if your estate is valued at or more than $2 million, then it makes sense to create a trust for the sole purpose of decreasing certain estate taxes. For this, you should seek the services of a professional.

F.   What a Will Cannot Do for You

Limitations on a will are things in your will that, no matter what you write, will not be enforced by the courts. The main limitations on a will are that a will cannot be used to conduct illegal activity and cannot put unreasonable conditions on inheriting property.

Illegal activity is anything that is unlawful to do in the state where the will is probated. Any provision in your will that violates a state or Federal law will be struck down. If too many of these provisions are included in your will, then a court might see this as evidence that you lacked a "sound mind" when you created your will, especially if the provisions are obvious in their illegality.

You are allowed to put reasonable conditions and restraints on an inheritance. For example, you can instruct your executor to only pay your daughter if she graduates from college.

An example of an unreasonable restraint is a restriction you write into your will that only allows a person to inherit if they do something that is against public policy, including permanently restricting a person's right to transfer, sell, or enjoy the property. So, if the executor can pay your daughter only if she agrees to divorce her husband, that is an unreasonable restraint and the provisions will be ignored by the courts.

Permanent restrictions on inheritance in a will are not allowed. For example, if you will your car to your neighbor only if he agrees to never drive it on a Sunday, the court will not allow this provision in your will. However, you may include a restriction if you include a time limit on the restriction. So, if instead you write that your neighbor is not allowed to drive the car on Sundays for the next year that may be allowed because it is not an absolute restriction on your neighbor's ownership of the car.

Pets are more than animals, they are family members. Therefore, it is only natural for people to want to leave their property to their pets. However, you cannot leave money or property to a pet because, in the eyes of the law, an animal cannot own property. There are ways of working around that. For example, you can leave money or property to a family member or friend with the condition that it be used to take care of your pets. If you set up a trust with a named executor to distribute funds to take care of your pets, the law will allow you to do that.

States that allow trusts for pets: Alaska, Arizona, Arkansas, California, Colorado, Washington, D.C., Florida, Hawaii, Idaho, Illinois, Iowa, Kansas, Maine, Michigan, Missouri, Montana, Nebraska, Nevada, New Hampshire, New Jersey, New Mexico, New York, North Carolina, Oregon, Tennessee, Texas, Utah, Washington (State), Wisconsin, and Wyoming.

G. Effects of Marital Status on Your Will

Marital status can usually be defined as single, married, or divorced. However, if you are going through a transitional phase, such as a separation or a court sanctioned separation which is ongoing at the time of your death, your state's laws may probate your will as if you are married. This means that your surviving spouse will receive their legal share of your estate, regardless of what you have written in your will. Also, if your divorce is pending (has not been finalized by the courts), or you are going through an annulment at the time of death, your relationship with your spouse will be defined as "married" under the law and your property will be distributed according to the marriage laws of the state.

Another possibility is that your relationship may be defined, under the law, as a common law marriage. *Common law marriage* is the union between two people that has not been formalized using the normal methods as prescribed by law, but is created by agreement to marry followed by cohabitation. For the purposes of probating your will, the court will consider you married if you are in a common law marriage in a state that recognizes common law marriages. Common law marriages are only recognized in certain states.

Note: to end a common law marriage, a spouse must formally file papers of a normal divorce. There is no separate divorce process for common law marriages. You cannot get out of a common law marriage simply by ending the cohabitation.

Common law marriages are recognized in: Alabama, Colorado, Washington, D.C., Georgia (only if created prior to January 1, 1997), Idaho (only if created prior to January 1, 1996), Iowa,

Kansas, Montana, New Hampshire (only for inheritances), Ohio (only if created prior to October 10, 1991), Oklahoma, Pennsylvania (only if created prior to January 1, 2005), Rhode Island, South Carolina, Texas, and Utah.

H.   How to Change an Existing Will

For most people, writing a will is not a one-time event. You should review your will periodically and consider whether you need to make any changes to reflect any new property that you have acquired. Also, reviewing your will can give you a chance to make changes if your wishes have changed. In addition, you should update your will following certain events, such as:

- a change in your marital status, such as if you get married, divorced, or remarried,
- the birth and/or adoption of children, from current or previous marriage(s), and/or grandchildren,
- the death of a parent, spouse, child, or anyone named in the will,
- if you make the decision to take someone out of your will,
- significant financial losses, gains, or if you incur any new debts,
- if you change your state of residence, or
- if you buy property in another state.

You can change your will after it has been signed and witnessed. There are several ways to make the changes, but the easiest way is to create a new will. In the new will, include a statement that all prior wills are superseded by this new will. Another way to make changes to your will is to create a *codicil*. A codicil is a separate document containing a statement of the changes to your will. A codicil can be used to change a single part of the will or multiple parts. With modern technology, it is easy to create a new will or create a codicil.

Failure to change your will can have unintended consequences. For example, if all of the people in your will are now dead, then your property will be distributed according to state law, which usually means the property will go to your relatives, and your wishes may not be fulfilled. If you have children after your will is created and your children are not named in your will because it has not been changed, then the court will decide who will care for your children. Keep in mind that any matters you do not address in your will may have to be addressed by your survivors who will incur the costs of litigating these matters, at their expense.

I.   Handwritten Wills

Remember there is no requirement that your will be typed. One option is to handwrite your will, called a *holographic will*. Witnesses are not required to be valid in most jurisdictions, but your holographic will must:

- be completely in your own handwriting (partially in your handwriting and partially in another's handwriting or typed with your initials above are generally not accepted),
- be signed and dated by you, and
- include a clear statement that it is your intention to make this your will.

Also remember that holographic wills are greatly disfavored by the courts and you should only create one if it is your only option. If it is possible to create a typed will, it is best that you do so.

J. Simultaneous Death

Simultaneous death is a rare occurrence. *Simultaneous death* is the legal term for when both spouses die within a very short period from one another. A minority of states follow the rule that, if one spouse outlives the other, even by a few minutes or seconds, the last in time to survive will have their will govern the estate of both spouses. This can be problematic if it's hard to determine which spouse died last.

To alleviate this problem, many states have enacted a *Uniform Simultaneous Death Act*, which alleviates the problem of having to determine which spouse died last in time, so long as both spouses die within the specified amount of time set out by state law. Where both spouses die within the specified amount of time from one another, the law considers each to have predeceased (died before) the other i.e., each spouse is considered to have died before the other spouse. All the property of one spouse will pass to the other spouse.

For example, New York's simultaneous death statute defines simultaneous death as one spouse dying within 72 hours of the other spouse. What that means is that, for will purposes, if one spouse dies within 72 hours of the other spouse, and New York law governs the estate, then all the property of the first spouse will be legally owned by the second spouse at the time of death.

Simultaneous deaths become an issue when the husband names his wife as his sole beneficiary and the wife names the husband as her sole beneficiary. In that case, each is said to have died before the other. In this case, both estates are divided up by a probate judge and the property distributed among the beneficiaries.

One way to avoid your state's simultaneous death statute is to include a survivorship provision in your will. A *survivorship provision* is a statement in your will stating one spouse must survive the other for a specified period of time before the property of the deceased spouse can pass to the other spouse. Since you can make the time greater than the simultaneous death statute time period, you can avoid this unintended consequence of your named beneficiaries not inheriting your property. The time period must be a limited and reasonable period of time. Therefore, even if the husband and wife die "simultaneously" under the statute, the husband would not take the wife's property because of the survivorship requirement in her will and the property would pass to the wife's beneficiaries.

If both husband and wife include a survivorship provision in their will, and die simultaneously, then the court will make a determination as what to do according to state law and the facts of the situation. It is better to have a survivorship provision in your will so you have the best chance of having your wishes honored.

It is worth noting, again, that simultaneous deaths are rare occurrences.

K. Dying Without a Will

When a person dies without a will, they are referred to as having died *intestate*. If you do not create a will, the court will appoint a special representative who will distribute your property according to the laws of the state.

It's important to note that any property you own, but which is not included in your will is distributed by the special representative.

L. Taxes

Taxes are an important consideration. Only really large estates have complex tax returns to file, but other estates will likely need to file taxes with the Federal and state governments. There are ways to reduce your tax burden, but not many, if any, ways to avoid taxes all together. There is generally a tax payer. All estates should file taxes and be paid before any property is distributed. If your estate is below the minimum amount required to file taxes, it is still advisable to file taxes so the government can take you off of their tax rolls. Filing taxes lets the government know that you have died and filing taxes is a good way to be checked off their list and avoid estate problems.

The money to pay taxes comes from your property, unless you have a surviving spouse who will be liable for taxes that are due. Even after you die, your estate may continue to generate income or losses from bank accounts and other investments. These gains and losses need to be reported to the government.

After you die, your executor (referred to by the IRS as a personal representative) must file a personal income tax return for the year that you died (January 1st until your death). Also, anyone that receives property from your estate, including a trustee and beneficiaries, will need to report the gains on their income taxes.

Both Federal and state governments tax an estate, but in different ways. State taxes can vary greatly between jurisdictions.

a) Federal Taxes

There are three possible Federal tax returns that need to be filed by your estate (all three may not be required):

- **Final income tax return,** (also referred to as the *individual income tax return*), IRS Form 1040, is required only if the deceased person earned more than the minimum amount of income in the year of death. As of the date of this book, that amount is income greater than $9,750 for a single person under 65 years of age, $11,200 for persons over 65 years of age, and $19,500 for married couples filing jointly plus $1,150 for each spouse aged 65 or older. It is due April 15 of the year following death.

- **Trust income tax return,** IRS Form 1041, is required if there is a trust and the trust receives more than a minimum amount of income. As of the date of this book, that amount is income $600 or greater. This tax return is not required if the minimum income is not met or you're the surviving spouse and inherited your spouse's property through a trust that leaves everything to you in a revocable living trust (you will report income gains or losses from the assets on your individual tax returns). It is due April 15 of the year following death, but in some cases, you can choose a different reporting period.

- **Estate tax return,** IRS Form 706, is required if the person died with more than the amount excluded from estate tax. This is required only for very large estates. As of the date of this book, that amount is greater than $5.12 million of taxable income. It is due nine months following death.

In addition to taxes on your estate, there might be penalties. IRS penalties can add up quickly. First, failure to file a return incurs a penalty of 5% of the tax due for each month a return is late, up to a maximum of 25%. Also, failure to pay the tax is penalized at 0.5% for each month the tax isn't paid. This has no maximum cap.

b) State Taxes

In addition to Federal taxes, state taxes may also need to be paid by your estate. If your estate has any state taxes that are due, the executor will need to file the state tax return and pay the tax before making distributions. The possible state tax returns include:

- **Final state income tax return** which is required if the deceased person earned more than a minimal amount of income in the year of death, as determined by the state. It is due April 15 of the year following death.

- **State trust income tax return** which is required if there is a trust and the trust receives more than a minimum amount of income. The due date will depend on state law.

- **State estate tax return** which is required if the estate is large enough. The amount varies between $675,000 and $3.5 million, depending on state law. The due date will also depend on state law. States with estate taxes are: Connecticut, Delaware, Hawaii, Illinois, Maine, Maryland, Massachusetts, Minnesota, New Jersey, New York, North Carolina (repealed for deaths as of January 1, 2013), Ohio (repealed for deaths as of January 1, 2013), Oregon, Rhode Island, Tennessee (repealed for deaths as of January 1, 2013), Vermont, Washington (State), and Washington, D.C.

- **State inheritance tax return** which is required if the state imposes it. The due date will depend on state law. The inheritance tax is dependent on the relationship of the beneficiary to the deceased. Spouses are always exempt from inheritance tax. Other beneficiaries pay depending on how close they were to the deceased person. There may be one tax rate for lineal descendants (e.g., children, grandchildren) and another rate for everyone else. Inheritance tax is imposed by the deceased person's state regardless of where the new owner lives. States with inheritance taxes include: Indiana (20%), Iowa (15%), Kentucky (16%), Maryland (10%), Nebraska (18%), New Jersey (16%), Pennsylvania (15%), and Tennessee (9.5%).

M. Probate Court

Probate court is a court that handles primarily estate administration such as validating a will, distributing property, and naming guardians if required. Your will must be filed in probate court by your executor or a family member. The court will determine if your will is valid, then your property will be collected by the executor you chose, and then the court will distribute your property after all debts and taxes have been paid. This determination by the court is known as *probate*. A will is not legally binding until it goes through probate. The exact process of probating a will can vary greatly from court to court. It can only take place after your death. Probate is sometimes called *estate administration*.

a) What Property Goes Through Probate?

In probate there are two types of property; probate property and non-probate property.

Probate property is property that you own at the time of your death that is specifically named to beneficiaries in your will. If your will does not mention a property that you own at the time of your death or you have not created a will, then your property will be distributed according to state law.

Non-probate property is property that you do not own at the time of your death, and is, therefore, not subject to probate. Examples of non-probate property include life insurance (on your life) payable to beneficiaries, a trust (containing your property) with named beneficiaries, or any joint property you own with rights of survivorship.

Although the categories may seem elementary, categorizing your property before you make your will makes it easier to identify what property is not part of your will. A will does not control non-probate property. Naming non-probate property in your will has no effect on the property. Therefore, if you do name non-probate property in your will, it will not pass according to your will. While probate property is required to be distributed through probate court, non-probate does not. The named beneficiary of non-probate property can get the property distributed to them by proving to the person or organization that is in possession of the property that you have died.

b) How to Avoid Probate Court

There are many ways to avoid your property having to go through probate court. Some of them are discussed throughout the book. Although not a complete list, ways of avoiding probate that are discussed in this book are:

- *joint tenancy with right of survivorship*— property owned by two or more people with the understanding that the last one of them to live will take all of the property, and the others (who die before any of the others) take nothing,
- *community property*—in a community property state, each spouse brings into the marriage one-half of all property acquired by either spouse during the marriage,
- *pay on death accounts*—an account (often bank accounts, securities, real estate deeds, and car registration) that passes to a designated beneficiary upon the death of the owner,
- life insurance,
- retirement accounts,
- trusts, and
- you can give your property away as gifts during your lifetime.

N. Next Steps to Creating Your Will

Now that you have a basic understanding of what a will is and how creating a will can be beneficial for you, the next step is to understand who can receive your property upon your death. Not everyone is the same under the eyes of the law. A person's relationship to you, may determine how much of your property they must inherit. After you identify the person you would like to leave property to, you can identify the property you wish to leave them.

3. Identifying the People in Your Will

O nce you understand the basic functions of a will, your next step is to understand how someone can be named in your will. Certain people, because of their special relationship to you, must be named in your will. In this chapter, you will learn about the different people who you can give your property to in your will.

A. People in Your Will are Beneficiaries

Any person or organization that you name in your will, or is included under the terms of documents such as insurance policies or retirement accounts, is called a *beneficiary*. If you do not have a will, the law dictates that certain members of your family inherit your property. Family members who inherit your property are called *heirs*.

The four main categories of beneficiaries that you should be aware of are:

a) primary beneficiaries,
b) alternate beneficiaries,
c) residuary beneficiaries, and
d) alternate residuary beneficiaries.

Certain states require that you mention your spouse and children in your will, even if you do not leave them anything, as a way of showing that you were of "sound mind" when you created the will.

a) Primary Beneficiaries

A *primary beneficiary* is the person you choose to receive property. If they are named in your will, then you have chosen them to receive property. You can have one primary beneficiary who will receive all of your property, or you can have multiple primary beneficiaries. If you want to give different people or organizations different things, once you name them in your will, they are all primary beneficiaries. You do not have to leave them equal shares of your property. All primary beneficiary must be specifically mentioned in your will along with the property you want them to receive. If they are not mentioned, they are not a primary beneficiary.

You can name multiple people and instruct them to share a single property. See below for considerations in naming shared beneficiaries. As a general rule, naming percentages of property is favored over using dollar amounts. This helps avoid the consequences of fluctuations in prices where inflation can play a part in property value that is not in cash form. If you use dollar amounts, and the property value falls below the amount that you have specified, the court may seek to satisfy the dollar amount by supplementing from elsewhere in the estate which can have the unintended consequence of giving a lesser share of your estate to another beneficiary. A percentage, on the other hand, will remain relative to the value. So, even if the value drops, the percentage will not change. Make sure that if you do split your property into percentages, that the sum of all the percentages equals 100%.

b)   Alternate Beneficiaries

Just as the primary beneficiary is your first choice to receive property when you die, the *alternate beneficiary* is the person or organization you choose to act as an alternative to receive your property in the event that the primary beneficiary dies prior to your death or does not want the property. The alternate beneficiary is your second choice. Naming an alternate beneficiary is not required, but many people choose to name one because it's good planning. Also, naming an alternate beneficiary keeps you from having to make another will if a primary beneficiary dies before you do.

You can name property to be shared between two or more people. You can name alternate beneficiaries to any of those receiving shared property. For example, if the property is a rare book and 50% ownership is left to friend A, by name, and the other 50% is left to friend B, by name, you can still name an alternative to friend A or to friend B. If a beneficiary has predeceased you and you don't name an alternative beneficiary, the property will pass by state law. It may go to the other friend, to a family member, or to the residuary beneficiary. The *residuary beneficiary* is the beneficiary who receives any remaining property of the estate that you owned at the time of death not left to anyone else in the will or otherwise.

The alternate beneficiary does not have to be a person; it can be an organization. Note that naming a human, primary beneficiary does not mean that you cannot name an organization as an alternate beneficiary, or vice versa. You are free to select any combination you want. The alternate beneficiary must be named as an alternate beneficiary in your will along with the property to be transferred.

You can also name an alternate beneficiary for the alternate beneficiary. For example, you can leave your house to friend A, in the event of A's death, the house goes to B, in the event of B's death the house goes to C. You can name as many alternate beneficiaries as you want. Naming multiple, alternate beneficiaries is uncommon because naming a primary and an alternate is usually enough, and the residuary beneficiary will take the remainder of the property if the primary and alternate are not available. One additional alternate may be reasonable under certain circumstances. In general, though, you only need to name one alternate for each major piece of property you own, such as a house.

When you name an alternate beneficiary, you can specify the period of time the alternate beneficiary must live before they can take ownership of the property. The period is known as a *survivorship period.* (See also simultaneous death.)

For example, you can name your best friend as your primary beneficiary with a 30 day survivorship period and a different friend as your alternate beneficiary. So, if you die on January 1, and the primary beneficiary lives past January 31, then the primary beneficiary will inherit. But, if your primary beneficiary dies on January 15, then they will not have lived past the 30 day survivorship period and so your alternate beneficiary will inherit. Why can survivorship periods be important? If you die on January 1 and then your primary beneficiary dies on January 15, and you have not written a survivorship period clause, then your property would go to your primary beneficiary who has died and then the property will pass according to their will, bypassing your wishes.

c)   Residuary Beneficiaries

The *residuary beneficiary* is the person or organization who inherits the remainder of your estate that you do not mention in your will or give away elsewhere. The reason a residual beneficiary exists in the law, is because it is very difficult to name everything that you own. The residuary beneficiary is named in your will, but no property needs to be described. Anything left over after all specific property has been distributed (to the primary and/or alternate beneficiaries) will go to the residuary beneficiary.

You can name more than one residuary beneficiary by saying, for example, that you want 50% of the residuary estate to go to your son, residuary 1, and the other 50% to your daughter, residuary 2. See below section *Naming Shared Beneficiaries*.

d)   Alternate Residuary Beneficiaries

Just like the alternate beneficiary, the *alternate residuary beneficiary* takes the place of the residuary beneficiary if the residuary beneficiary dies before you. Naming an alternative residuary beneficiary is not required, but, if you want to name one, you must do so by using specific language. You can also name a survivorship period for the alternate residuary beneficiaries.

B. Charitable Organizations and the Government as Beneficiaries

Many people choose to name charitable organizations as beneficiaries. Charitable organizations include nonprofits as well as houses of worships, e.g. the American Red Cross, your local food bank, temples, and churches. However, there are certain limitations you should keep in mind when you name one of these organizations as a beneficiary in your will.

If you choose to leave a large amount of money to a charitable organization, many states place a time limit prior to death, when you are not allowed to change your will to exclude the charity. The states created these time limits in order to notify the charity that they will not receive the large sum that they may have depended on and to give that charity time to look for funding elsewhere to make up for the amount of money you are no longer giving them. Your state rules will govern exactly what you can do. If a charity is relying on your future gift, the money or property you left to that charity in your will, and you change your will without telling that charity, the charity may be able to successfully sue your estate for that money after you die. And so, to prevent these kinds of confusions and lawsuits, it is important that you carefully consider what charity/charities you want to name in your will and how much you want to leave to them.

Most states place a limit on how much of your estate you can give to charity; the limit is usually around 50%. The reason certain states have such a limit is to prevent people from giving away all of their property in the hopes that they will be forgiven for past conduct at the expense of taking from their heirs.

Some people want to leave money to the government that is not in the form of taxes. You are allowed to do that. You can leave money to the United States and that money will go to the Federal government. You can also specifically leave money to a state or local government.

C. Naming Shared Beneficiaries

The biggest concern you should have when naming a shared beneficiary is the potential conflicts that come with shared ownership.

It can be difficult for multiple beneficiaries to share the same property. This is especially true when the property is something like a house where the property cannot be divided into pieces. If you choose to leave a single piece of property, like a house, to multiple beneficiaries, it is helpful to also describe the percentage of the property that each beneficiary will own.

If you name multiple beneficiaries, but do not mention their share of ownership, the court will assume each is to get an equal share. If you do name a relative share to the beneficiaries, you can name disproportionate shares. For example you can give 25% ownership to one beneficiary and 75% to the other. If you do not want your will to operate this way, you should seek resources outside of this book.

D. Who Cannot Be a Beneficiary

There are certain people who cannot inherit as a beneficiary, even if they are expressly named in your will. These people are disqualified from being beneficiaries in your will. If a disqualified beneficiary is named in your will the court will not honor your wishes regarding the distribution to the disqualified beneficiary and the property will pass to the next person eligible to inherit as set out in your will or by state law.

The following are disqualified beneficiaries:

- anyone involved in creating the will,

    - including the attorney who drafted your will because it would be assumed that the attorney participated only so they would be included in your will.
    - generally, states do not allow anyone who serves as a witness to your will to be named as a beneficiary. It is much safer to not have any beneficiaries act as witnesses.

- anyone who murders you,

    - this just makes practical sense. If someone named in your will kills you, then the killer, and anyone who participates in your killing, is disqualified from being your beneficiary.

- generally, states do not allow unincorporated associations to be named as a beneficiary in your will,

    - an *unincorporated association* is a general partnership that is not registered with the state but is acting as a business entity.

- any for-profit corporations,

- animals (but remember that you can leave money in a trust to pay for the care of your animals), or

- minors.

- either the court will appoint a guardian or you can appoint someone to manage the property until they are legally an adult.
- minors require adult supervision to inherit property. You can appoint a specific person to manage the property until the minor reaches the age of majority. If you do not appoint an adult supervisor, the court will appoint a guardian.

E. Disinheriting Spouses, Children, and Others

Disinheriting someone means that you want to keep them from getting your property when you die. People that you want to disinherit fall into three categories: spouses, children, or others.

Spouses are difficult to disinherit. In most states, you are not allowed to disinherit a spouse. If you are married at the time of death, then by law, your spouse is entitled to receive a certain portion of your estate. Until a divorce has been finalized, you must account for the surviving spouse's shares or the court will take property in your estate given to other beneficiaries to satisfy the spouses share.

If you are divorced at the time of your death then most states do not require that you leave anything to the surviving divorced spouse. States are for the most part, common law states, meaning that you cannot legally disinherit a spouse that has not been divorced at the time of marriage. The other states are community property states, meaning that most of the property that is acquired during the marriage is owned together by each of the spouses. In both common law states and community property states, if you are married at the time of your death, then you should leave one-half of your estate to the surviving spouse. If you fail to do so, then the spouse might be able to get more than half from your estate, depending on how the court rules.

Children can be disinherited, but you must do so with specific language. Just failing to mention your children will not be enough to disinherit them. But, if you leave your child a very small amount, such as one dollar, that child will be considered disinherited. Minor children cannot be disinherited, but those over 18 can be disinherited with specific language.

Others can be easily disinherited by not naming them in the will. That would include your siblings, parents, grandchildren, and friends. There is no need to leave one dollar because they are not entitled to anything if they are not mentioned.

F. What Happens If the Beneficiary Rejects the Property?

It's very rare that someone rejects an inheritance, so rare that most people don't think about it because, generally, no one rejects property given in a will. Acceptance of an inheritance is assumed, unless action is taken to reject the gift in the will. A beneficiary can reject an inheritance by informing the executor or the court appointed special representative of their desire not to receive the property.

There are a few reasons why a beneficiary might not want the property. For example, a person may reject property to avoid negative tax consequences. Some people don't want the hassle of dealing with out of state property.

Whatever the reason, a beneficiary has the right to reject property by stating their rejection clearly at the time the will is probated.

When a named beneficiary rejects property, the property passes to the alternate beneficiary, the residuary, the alternate residuary beneficiary, and then according to state law.

G. Guardians for Minor Child(ren)

A *personal guardian* is, by definition, someone other than a legal parent who will be responsible for raising minor child(ren) in the event that the legal parents die. A personal guardian cannot take the place of a living legal parent, but only takes care of the child(ren) should both of the parents die. Courts are generally very reluctant to separate a child from their parents, especially following the death of one of the parents.

When deciding who to name as a personal guardian for your child(ren) in your will, remember that the person you name could be raising your child(ren). The personal guardian must be an adult of at least 18 years of age. You should consider how likely it is that the person you name will accept the responsibility and whether or not you can trust that person to act in the best interest of child(ren). The personal guardian you name in your will does not have to accept the responsibility and is not bound until they agree in court and a judge appoints them as the legal guardian of the minor child(ren). Along with naming a personal guardian, it is common to name an alternate guardian in your will.

When you name a personal guardian for your child(ren), you should include a clause in your will stating your reasons for naming that person. You should also include a similar clause for why you chose the alternate guardian. These clauses can help the court in a situation where there is conflict about who should get the child(ren).

It is important that both parents name the same personal guardians and alternate personal guardians to avoid conflicts about who will take care of the minor child(ren) in the case of simultaneous death.

Custody requests in your will are not automatically honored. A judge will make the final determination as to what is in the best interests of your minor child(ren).

Sometimes you may need to name different personal guardians for your child(ren), i.e. split up the child(ren). This is only done in extremely rare cases, but it can be done with a clause that specifically states your intention to name separate personal guardians for each child. It is helpful to describe the reasons why you believe it is in the best interest of the child(ren) to have different personal guardians.

You do not need to appoint a personal guardian for any child (ren) who have reached 18 years of age. If you have a child who requires special care, such as a special needs child, please seek additional resources from a lawyer on ways to ensure they get the best care.

H. Witnesses

Two witnesses are required for a will to be valid in every state, except for Vermont which requires three witnesses. The legal requirement for witnesses is often overlooked by those creating a will, but without witnesses a will cannot be enforceable. There is no requirement that you know the witnesses.

The rules about witnesses are different in every state. For example, there are some states that allow a witness to a will to be under the age of 18 and some states allow a witness to be a beneficiary. While following the laws in your state is recommended, the trend in the law, in all states is to require a witness to be a non-beneficiary who is over the age of 18. To avoid the risk of a change in law, it's advisable that all witnesses to your will be non-beneficiaries who are over the age of 18.

I. Executor

The *executor* (also referred to as *personal representative*) is the person that you choose to complete the "winding up" of your estate, according to your will. The executor will take charge of your property through the probate process, or other means, and distribute your property according to your will. The entire process usually takes around six months to two years to complete, depending on the specifics of your situation and applicable state laws. If you do not name an executor, or the executor and the alternate executor that you name die before you, the court will appoint an administrator.

The executor is entitled to be paid for their services. State laws will generally suggest a standard of reasonable compensation, the amount of which will be dependent upon how much work the executor is expected to do on your estate's behalf. Your will is generally not expected to describe in hourly detail, the projected amount of work the executor will do, but, will usually state a lump sum or a percentage of the estate that will be the executor's compensation. However, it is not uncommon for an executor to accept no compensation and simply take on the responsibility out of love, or as a last gesture of kindness.

You can name anyone to be your executor, including beneficiaries. In fact, most people name a spouse or adult child who is going to get the majority of the property as the executor. This is perfectly legal. Be careful to consider whether your choice in executor will cause or enflame any familial conflicts. Instead of a family member, you can choose to name a friend or other third party, such as a lawyer, CPA, bank, or a trust to act as your beneficiary. Remember that certain professionals will need to be compensated for their services.

Prior to naming your executor and alternate executor in your will, you should discuss your decision with the people you want to choose and decide whether they are likely to act responsibly. Trust is the key. You don't want to name an executor that won't fulfill their duties, or worse. It is best to have a candid conversation with your potential executor(s) about your expectations and how you want your property to be distributed.

The executor is not required to keep any beneficiary informed about what the executor does in relation to the property in the estate, i.e. the executor can take whatever action the executor thinks is appropriate without having to consult or even inform beneficiaries before or after the actions occur. While there are limited legal actions your beneficiaries can take if your executor does not listen to the beneficiaries, as long as the actions of the beneficiary are reasonable, the executor is left to do their job. For the most part, the executor is given broad discretion to do the executor's job in a competent manner.

Naming co-executors is beyond the scope of this book because of the multitude of state specific, special rules relating to co-executors. For example, there might be a requirement that the co-executors agree before they can take any action which can make the process longer, and potentially more frustrating, if there is a fundamental disagreement.

You should name an executor and an alternate executor in your will. The duties of the executor will likely include:

- **Gathering the property of the testator and prepare an inventory.** This means getting all of the paperwork in order, collecting items that would be in danger of falling into disrepair such as a car, and monitoring bank accounts and investments.

- **Taking care of the property until it is time to hand it over to the beneficiaries.** This means that the executor will be responsible for any upkeep of your property and taking care of the house until it is time to distribute it. It does not mean that the executor has to perform physical labor, only that the executor will do what is in the best interest of the property to ensure the property is not damaged before it is distributed to your beneficiaries. Any executor acting in the best interest of the property may hire a gardener, make financial decisions, or decisions related to any businesses that are named in the will. These expenses are paid out of the estate's property before distribution to beneficiaries.

- **Selling any property that needs to be sold.** You can choose to instruct the executor of your will to sell your property and distribute the proceeds to your beneficiaries. If you choose for the executor to sell your property, they will be responsible for finding buyers and getting fair market value for the property. Note that certain states require the executors to get prior approval from the court before selling real estate.

- **Hiring attorneys and other professionals.** Where the estate requires a skill set that is beyond the scope of the executor's skill set or expertise, and the estate would likely benefit from the services of a professional, the executor is responsible for hiring and paying professionals. For example, if it is a large estate and the executor reasonably believes the estate would benefit from a tax attorney or accountant, then the executor can retain professional services which are paid from estate property.

- **Paying debts and taxes.** All property that is transferred by your will must be transferred after having paid any debts and taxes owed on that property. The executor is not personally liable for any debts and taxes, but the executor is responsible for filing the applicable paperwork on your estate's behalf. Generally, this means paying one year's taxes.

- Note: You cannot inherit someone else's debt. A person's property will be sold to pay off their debts: first, funeral and probate court costs, second, whatever funds are left, if any, will be used to pay off any remaining debts attached to the estate. If the remaining funds are not enough to cover the estate's outstanding debts, and there is no more property in the estate, then the creditors are out of luck and cannot come after the beneficiaries. In some states, the creditors must go through probate to force the sale of property to collect on a debt. If the testator has distributed their property in a way that eliminates the need for probate, then the creditors cannot gain access to that property. If there is no property to sell to settle the testator's debts, those debts will be wiped out.

- **Paying off secured debts may not be required.** Debts secured by property, such as a mortgage or vehicle loan, are called *secured debts* or *liens*. Generally, secured debts do not have to be paid off before the property is distributed because banks may allow the beneficiary to take over your loan, but it is the bank's decision. If the bank does not transfer over the loan to your beneficiary, then the beneficiary has the option to pay off the debt with the money the beneficiary has personally, can apply for a new loan with their credit secured by the house, or allow the bank to sell the property and collect the balance after the loan and fees are paid. Banks rarely exercise this power and allow the new owner to continue under the existing loan. If you want your estate to pay off the secured debts before transferring to the beneficiary, you need to state your wishes in your will.

- **Distributing the property when it is time to do so.** The distribution of the testator's property will occur after probate. If the property is non-probate property, the executor can distribute that property immediately or in a reasonable amount of time.

- **Distributing the remaining property according to the will or by state law.** Once the will has been settled and/or probated, and the property is distributed to the beneficiaries, any property not distributed will be given to the named residuary beneficiary or distributed according to state law.

To guarantee that the executor will not waste the money and property in the estate, you may want to require that your executor post a bond. Where a will states that a bond is not required, a court, generally, will not require one. If your will does not state a bond requirement, the court may require the executor to post a bond before the court will approve the will. If the executor is an out of state resident, the court may impose a bond regardless of what is in the will.

Out of state executors are often not allowed by state law in order for the state to ensure it keeps jurisdiction over the executor. The executor has broad control over the estate. By requiring an in-state executor, the courts have jurisdiction over the executor which may prevent dishonesty on behalf of the executor. For that reason, most states will not allow an out of state executor. Even where allowed, naming an out of state executor can have some unintended restrictions:

- **Alabama.** Out of state residents can serve as executors in Alabama only if the property in Alabama is part of an estate which includes property located in the executor's estate.

- **Florida.** Out of state residents can only serve as executors in Florida only if they are legally related to the testator by blood or marriage.

- **Iowa.** Out of state residents can serve as executors in Iowa only if there is named a co-executors who is a residents of Iowa, or where the court approves the out of state executors to serve alone.

- **Kentucky.** Out of state residents can only serve as executors in Kentucky only if they are legally related to the testator by blood or marriage.

- **Nevada.** Out of state residents can serve as executors in Nevada only if there is named a co-executors who is a resident of Nevada.

- **Ohio.** Out of state residents can only serve as executors in Ohio only if they are legally related to the testator by blood or marriage or the out of state residents is from a state that allows out of state residents to serve as executors.

- **Pennsylvania.** Out of state residents can only serve as executors after getting permission from the register of wills which the executor gets by filing out an affidavit stating that the deceased has no debt in Pennsylvania, and that the executor will not engage in any conduct that is prohibited in the executor's state of residence.

- **Tennessee.** Out of state residents can only serve as executors in Tennessee if they are legally related to the testator or only if there is named a co-executor who is a resident of Tennessee.

- **Vermont.** Out of state residents can only serve as executors in Vermont if the court approves a request for approval made by the surviving spouse, adult children, or the parents or legal guardians of minor children.

J. Next Steps to Creating Your Will

Now that you have an idea about how people can receive your property and how to classify those people in your will, the next chapter will teach you how to identify and classify the property that you will leave to people in your will.

4. Identifying the Property in Your Will

After you have identified the people you would like to include in your will, the next natural thing to do is to identify the property you would like to leave those people in your will. Understanding how your property is owned is the key to classifying your property. Classifying your property will help you decide how to distribute the property in your will. In this chapter, you will identify how property is owned and then learn how you want your property distributed in your will.

A. What Property Can Be Distributed by Will?

You can leave any property that you own, at the time of your death, to someone in your will. If you no longer own the property because you sold it or have given it away, then it cannot be distributed in your will and the provision granting that property is void. So, if you decide to give away or sell a piece of property that you had previously named in your will the person you sold or gave your property to gets to keep it.

You are allowed to make specific gifts in your will. Giving someone a specific gift in your will is called a *specific bequest*. For example, you can will to your niece a specific, blue mirror.

The laws of the state of your permanent residence will, generally, apply to the property distributed according to your will. If the property distributed in your will is real estate in another state or country, the laws of the state or country where the real estate property sits will govern.

B.   What Property Cannot Be Distributed by Will?

Property in a trust. Property that is in a trust, including in a living trust, cannot be left in a will.

Accounts you've already named beneficiaries for. Insurance policies, retirement accounts, pension plans, and pay on death accounts in which you have already named beneficiaries cannot be distributed by will because the property is automatically distributed upon your death.

Shares of a business that you own. If you own transferable or inheritable shares of a business, then those shares, or income from those shares, can be left to a person in your will, but only to the extent that you own those shares and no more.

Joint tenancy property. An entirely separate category of property that cannot be distributed by will is property that is owned with another person in a joint tenancy with rights of survivorship. See next section, *How Can Property Be Owned*.

Money to animals. Any will provision that leaves property outright to an animal will not be followed because animals cannot own property.

C. How Can Property Be Owned?

Identifying and understanding how property is owned will help you determine how your property can be distributed in your will, if at all. In this section, you will learn about solely owned property, the different ways in which property can be jointly owned, and about the special rules that govern property that is acquired during a marriage.

a) Solely Owned Property

Solely owned property that you own by yourself, separate from even your spouse is the easiest to leave in your will. If the property is solely owned by you, then you can name the property in your will as a specific bequest. This is true regardless of whether there is any debt attached to it (such as a lien). If you do owe any debt on the property, the debt will need to be paid before the property passes because you cannot, generally, inherit another person's debts. But debts protected by a lien, such as a house mortgage or car loan, are called *secured debts*, and, generally, do not have to be paid off before the property is distributed. Although a bank legally has the final call if the secured debt is to be paid in full following the death of the secured debt owner. Banks rarely exercise this right and allow transfers of secured debts. If there is a default, then the bank can take the property.

b) Jointly Held Property

Jointly held property can present some unique challenges when you are trying to transfer the property in your will. Mainly, it presents a problem because you are not the sole owner and the rights of the other joint holder in the property should be considered.

States have three ways property can be jointly owned:

1) Tenancy in common,
2) Joint tenancy with right of survivorship, and
3) Tenancy by the entirety.

i.   Tenancy in Common

Tenancy in common is a term used to describe a type of ownership of property where a property is owned, jointly, with all of the joint holders of the property having a right to the use and enjoyment of the entire property, not just a portion of the land. However, each owner owns a percentage of the property that can be freely transferred, without approval from the other owners. In other words, you own the right to use all of the property in any way you choose, and you can sell your share without having to notify the other owners.

Where parties try to create a joint tenancy with rights of survivorship, but fail to do so, usually because of a failure to comply with legal formalities, a tenancy in common will be created. The tenancy in common is used by the courts as a default because judges favor the free transfer of property that the tenancy in common offers. See below *Joint Tenancy with Rights of Survivorship* section for more details.

If your state recognizes tenancy by the entirety for married couples, then spouses can own property together. See below *Tenancy by the Entirety* section for more details.

ii. Joint Tenancy with Rights of Survivorship

Property that is owed as *joint tenancy with rights of survivorship*, the property is owned by two or more people with the understanding that the last one of them to live owns all of the property. Where a joint tenancy with rights of survivorship is created, all *joint tenants*, the owners with the rights of survivorship, have a right to the use and enjoyment of the entire property. For example, Greenacre is owned by A, B, and C as joint tenants with rights of survivorship. Each owns one-third of Greenacre. C dies. Now, A owns one-half and B owns one-half. C's heirs have no interest in Greenacre. Now, B dies. A owns Greenacre. B and C's heirs have no interest in Greenacre.

Joint tenants can transfer their interest in the property by selling it. When one joint tenant sells their interest in a property, the new owner becomes a tenant in common with no rights of survivorship. For example, Blackacre is owned by A, B, and C as joint tenants with rights of survivorship. Each owns one-third of Blackacre. C sell's their interest to D. A and B still own one-third interest each in Blackacre as joint tenants, but now the remaining one-third share is owned by D as a tenant in common. That is because when C sold to D, C broke the joint tenancy and created a tenancy in common. Now, if C dies, D is still one-third owner as a tenant in common and, A and B remain joint tenants with rights of survivorship of the other two -third interest. C has no interest in Blackacre. Now, B dies. A owns two-thirds of Blackacre as a tenant in common with D, who owns the remaining one-third interest.

If, in the rare event, both joint tenants die simultaneously, each will be presumed to have predeceased the other and neither will take under a claim of survivorship. Both deceased will be treated as if they own one-third of the property and their shares will pass according to their will.

It is important to note that a joint tenancy with rights of survivorship is not favored by courts because it restricts the free transfer of property. So, to create a joint tenancy, you must use specific language by naming each joint tenant with their relative shares, and saying that you are all creating a "joint tenancy with the rights of survivorship." Check your state's rules as they may differ on the specific language required to create a joint tenancy. If specific language is not used, then a tenancy in common is created and not a joint tenancy with rights of survivorship.

If you create a joint tenancy with a right of survivorship in your will for others, for example, to your three children, be mindful of the potential for familial conflict.

Alaska does not recognize the joint tenancy with rights of survivorship.

iii. Tenancy by the Entirety

The *tenancy by the entirety* is a type of joint tenancy with rights of survivorship, but it can only be created between married couples, with the use of specific language that states that both spouses are creating a "tenancy by the entirety." Otherwise a tenancy in common is created. Laws regarding tenancy by the entirety vary greatly by state.

The primary difference between the joint tenancy with rights of survivorship and the tenancy by the entirety is that, in a tenancy by the entirety, one spouse cannot transfer interest in the property without consent of the other spouse. Creditors cannot attach interest to, and sell, a property without consent to attach an interest from both spouses.

You can only extinguishing a tenancy by the entirety by divorce, annulment, or by a joint agreement to amend any title property. At the death of one spouse, the surviving spouse takes full ownership of the property owned by a tenancy by the entirety.

In a tenancy by the entirety, both spouses have the right to enjoy all of the property.

States that allow tenancy by the entirety: Alaska (only for real estate), Arkansas, Connecticut, Delaware, Washington, D.C., Florida, Hawaii, Illinois (only for real estate), Indiana (only for real estate), Kentucky (only for real estate), Maryland, Massachusetts, Michigan, Mississippi, Missouri, New Jersey, New York (only for real estate), North Carolina (only for real estate), Ohio (only for real estate and if created before 4/4/1985), Oklahoma, Oregon (only for real estate), Pennsylvania, Rhode Island, Tennessee, Utah, Vermont, Virginia, and Wyoming.

c) Special Considerations for Marital Property

It is common for a spouse to leave most or all of their property to their surviving spouse. The law does not interfere with this. So long as you are distributing at least one-half of your estate to your spouse, there are, generally, no legal implications.

i.   How Can Marital Property Be Owned?

When you want to leave property to someone other than your surviving spouse, a judge will determine who the property belongs to, i.e. is the property yours to give away? This answer will depend on whether your state is a community property state or a common law property state.

Note that prenuptial agreements are valid contracts and may be binding on the couples who enter into them. If you entered into a prenuptial agreement with your spouse prior to your marriage, then the prenuptial agreement may dictate whether certain property is considered community property or not.

1.   Community Property States

Community property states are Alaska (only by written agreement), Arizona, California, Idaho, Nevada, New Mexico, Texas, Washington (State), and Wisconsin (a hybrid State where marital property law closely resembles community property states and covers all property owned at the time of death).

In a *community property state*, most property acquired during the marriage is owned equally (50%) by each spouse. Generally, if the property is acquired during the marriage, then it is community property, regardless of which spouse acquired it. For example, community property is:

- wages from employment and income earned by either spouse,
- property purchased from community property,

- gifts given to both spouses (which would include wedding gifts), and
- separate property which can be converted into community property if the separate property is mixed with community property so that what is separate and what is community property cannot be distinguished, or separate property that is converted into community property when the owner of the separate property converts the property into community property.

In a community property state, property that is owned by one spouse is either:

- their one-half share of community property that is owned together with the other spouse, or
- *separate property* which is defined as property acquired:
  - before the marriage,
  - during the marriage, or
    - with your own private, separate funds,
    - property purchased with the income from any property owned prior to the marriage that is sold because that income will be separate property (except in Washington state where it is considered community property),
    - gifts or inheritances received during the marriage but named specifically only to one spouse, or
    - community property converted into separate property by gift or written agreement.
  - after the marriage reaches a legal end.

For the most part, identifying what is community property and what is separate property will not be difficult. The vast majority of your property is community property. Here are the major problem areas:

- **Debts:** Personal debt not owned by the other spouse, will remain that spouse's individual responsibility. However, if one person in the marriage goes into debt acquiring necessities, such as food and/or shelter, that debt will be defined as marital debt. Necessities are a special category of things that are absolutely essential for life which can include food, shelter, and/or clothing. Often, the line between personal and community debt can be unclear.

- **Businesses:** If the business was owned by one of the spouses prior to the marriage, but continued during the marriage, any increase in the value of the business will likely be community property, but whether the remaining property is community property is not always clear.

- **Pensions:** Generally, pensions are community property. However, some, for example, Social Security retirement benefits and some other Federal pensions, are not. It is important to check your individual pension plan.

Usually, upon your death, one-half of all community property belongs to your surviving spouse. In your will, you may name your half of the community property in any way you choose.

2. Common Law Property States

States that are not community property states are *common law property states*. In a common law property state, individual property is:

- property purchased using income from employment and income earned separately from the other spouse, and
- property you own in only your name, so long as the property has ownership documents such as a deed or title.

If you use your personal income to purchase a house, but put your name and your spouse's name on the title, then both of you will own the house. If your spouse uses their personal funds to purchase a house, but only puts your name on the house, then you, not your spouse, own the house.

When a piece of property does not have a legal document that gives title to a named person, the property belongs to the person whose income was used to purchase that property. If the funds used to purchase a piece of property are jointly owned, then the property purchased with those funds is jointly owned.

In a common law property state, *separate property* is property held in only one of the spouse's names, regardless of who paid for the property.

In a common law property state, marital property is defined as property jointly owned by both spouses. So long as both names are on the title, or some other formal legal document, both spouses own the property no matter how the property was acquired.

ii. Spousal Shares

In almost every state, the surviving spouse is entitled to a share of the deceased spouse's share of property. Where a will fails to account for the surviving spouse's share, the court will take from the other beneficiaries to ensure that the surviving spouse gets their share. The percentage that the court will take from the other beneficiaries is called *elective shares*. In most states, elective shares range from one-third to one-half of all property in the estate that goes through probate, but some states will also include property that avoids probate. Some states will also consider whether the property is marital property or separate property.

As a rule of thumb, to be safe, you should leave 50% of your estate to your surviving spouse. If you want to provide less than the spousal share required by your state, then you will need to consult with a lawyer because that is beyond the scope of this book.

iii. Avoiding Spousal Shares

Spousal shares can be decreased by reducing the amount courts consider marital property.

One way to reduce your spouse's spousal share is to use of a prenuptial agreement that is signed prior to the marriage. A prenuptial agreement is a valid contract and is generally honored by courts, which allows spouses to decide their financial rights and responsibilities instead of state law and can protect against debts of the other spouse. The prenuptial agreement is entered into prior to the marriage. However, most states allow you to waive the prenuptial agreement by later showing your intent. Some states do not follow this rule.

Another way to decrease the amount of your spouse's spousal share is by a written agreement entered into by both spouses after the marriage to waive their share of the other spouse's estate. This is, generally, honored by courts, unless the surviving spouse can show that the document was signed under duress or coercion.

In some states, the spousal share can be decreased by owning the property in joint tenancy with someone other than the spouse or by placing the property into a trust. In some states, you can name someone other than your spouse in a life insurance policy.

D. Rules Governing Your Primary Home

The law commonly refers to your primary home as your *homestead,* and generally provides the homestead great protection. If you have a spouse and/or minor children, the laws in your state may not allow you to leave your homestead to anyone other than your spouse and/or minor children. If you are divorced, with minor children, then your homestead will be left to your children. In some states, the homestead is protected to the point that creditors can't attach to the house. It is also worth noting that creditors will not be able to attach to *exempt property,* which includes furniture, furnishings, appliances, and cars titled in your name that are regularly used by you, your spouse, and/or minor children. Exempt property first goes to the surviving spouse and then to the minor children.

E. Bank Accounts

The money in your bank account is considered property and will be subject to probate like any other property you own. There are ways of setting up bank accounts that will avoid probate.

Joint tenancy with right of survivorship: One way to guarantee that one person will inherit all of the funds in your bank account is to set up a joint tenancy with right of survivorship bank account. Just like joint tenancy with rights of survivorship of survivors in real property, the surviving owner will automatically get ownership of the entire account upon your death. Also, if you do create a joint tenancy, the other parties can take out as much money as they want without regard to how much they have contributed.

Payable on death bank accounts: If you have a specific person you would like to leave money to, creating a *payable on death bank account* is a great way of accomplishing that. This is a bank account that is kept separate from the rest of your estate, but within your exclusive control, until your death. The money you deposit in the bank account will be held in trust for the named beneficiary you choose. The account can be a checking, savings, money market, or certificate of deposit (CD) account. A payable on death account is created by filling out a form at the bank. Note that banks may use the term payable on death (POD), transfer on death (TOD), bank trust, or, the most commonly used term, *Totten trust*. You can think of this type of account as the most cost effective way of creating a trust.

Payable on death securities: Stocks, bonds, mutual funds, and other similar financial instruments can all be payable on death securities. The vast majority of states have passed a law called the Uniform TOD Securities Registration Act. To be valid, the security must be correctly registered. The brokerage firm that handles your account does the registration. If your state has not passed the law, you can move your securities into a state that has passed the law.

F. Life Insurance

If you name a beneficiary on your life insurance policy, it will not go through probate, but it will still be subject to estate taxes. The life insurance policy will pay directly to your named beneficiary. A life insurance policy is a contract between you and the insurance company where you promise to pay premiums and the insurance company promises to pay your named beneficiaries upon your death. Upon your death, your beneficiary will be required to fill out some paperwork and provide the insurance company a copy of your death certificate.

If you have named minor children as beneficiaries, generally, the life insurance policy will pay directly into a child's trust account. However, some insurance policies will not allow you to name minor children as beneficiaries, so it's important to check your insurance policy. If your insurance policy does not allow you to name minor children as beneficiaries then you can either:

- create a living trust, the beneficiaries of which are the minor children, and then name the living trust as the beneficiary of your life insurance policy, to be paid out immediately upon your death, or
- name a guardian to manage the property that will be inherited by the minor children.

Any life insurance proceeds will be subject to an estate tax. To avoid this, the life insurance policy will need to be owned by someone other than yourself (the decedent). For example, your daughter can purchase the policy on your behalf. Note that there may be certain gift tax consequences.

G. Property of Minor Children

If you have no surviving spouse, then your minor children will get the homestead as well as all of the furnishings in the house. Your minor children are also entitled to get a *family allowance*, which is controlled by state law. Money in a joint payable on death bank account is not part of a family allowance.

The problem is that, under the eyes of the law, minors are not allowed to own property without adult supervision. If you have minor children, you have to make the necessary arrangements to take care of your minor children, through a will or trusts, or the court will appoint someone, called a court-appointed guardian to do so. If the court makes the decisions, then a portion of your estate will be used to pay for the court appointed services.

When creating your will and/or trusts for your minor children, you must take into consideration the amount of money that you are leaving to them, and also money that the minor children will receive from life insurance policies, gifts, and/or retirement plans that name the children as beneficiaries.

H. Debt on the Property in the Will

When there is still debt owed on property that is distributed by your will then the loan will, generally, need to be paid off before the property can pass to the beneficiary. However, property secured with a lien on the property, for example a house mortgage or car loan, is not required to be paid off to be transferred to a beneficiary. Most companies who hold the mortgage or loan on a piece of property will allow the passing of debt to the new owner without requiring the new owner to refinance.

The debt on your property will be paid from other property in your estate in the following order: first, probate fees, taxes, and funeral costs, next any remaining debt. If you want to transfer property in your will free and clear of any debts, then you can have your estate pay the debt off by including a *debt-forgiveness clause*. Generally, if you do not specify which property is to be given free of debt, then the executor will have the power to make that decision. You can exercise control over this by naming the specific property you want to be given free of debt with the debt-forgiveness clause. If you give property with a secured lien debt attached to it to the beneficiary, that beneficiary does not have to accept the property and can disclaim the property by contacting the executor in writing.

If you set up your estate in such a way that your property does not have to go through probate, then creditors cannot touch your property and any debts remaining on the estate will be wiped out if there is no property to sell to settle the accounts.

Federal student debt is generally discharged on your death, which means that the property in your estate will not be used to pay off your student debt when you die. However, your executor will need to notify the lender by providing a death certificate. Private student debt is not so easily discharged and will need to be paid by the estate before property can be distributed.

The executor is not personally liable for the debts and taxes of your estate, but they are responsible for filing the paperwork on your behalf. Generally, this requires the executor to use estate funds to pay one year taxes of the deceased, unless the property is complicated or there is likely to be a dispute at probate by a family member.

I. Gifts

Before you die, you can gift your property to your beneficiaries. Any gift you make during your lifetime will not be subject to probate.

At the time of publication, Federal law allows an *annual exclusion* of gift tax, which is the amount you can give to someone in a calendar year (January 1 to December 31). You can gift up to $14,000 as a single giver free of Federal taxes and married couples can combine their gifts to give a joint gift of $28,000 in a calendar year. For example, you want to give $14,000 to A, that gift would be tax free so long as you have not reached your lifetime gift amount which is $5.35 million. Any amount over this amount or over the lifetime exclusion will be taxed around 40%. If you want to give A $14,000 on December 31, 2013 and the same amount to A on January 1, 2014, then this would still be free of Federal taxes so long as you were still within your lifetime limit of $5.35 million and did not make any other gifts. If you are married, you can give jointly up to $28,000 in a calendar year. The receiver of the gift does not pay gift taxes, but the person who makes the gift is the one who is taxed.

To qualify as a gift, there can be no strings or stipulations to the person who receives the money. It is their money and they can do what they want with it.

J. Retirement Accounts and Pensions

If, at the time of your death, there is any money left in your retirement account, your beneficiary will receive that money. The beneficiary should be registered with your brokerage house which creates a contract between you and the brokerage house which does not go through probate. If the brokerage house does not pay the beneficiary, then there is a breach of contract and your beneficiary can sue for nonpayment under contract law.

Retirement funds are subject to taxation. If you are considering naming someone other than your surviving spouse as a beneficiary, consult a lawyer or an accountant because the tax in this area can be complex.

Pension plans are not as common as they once were, although they do still exist. They are now called *defined benefit plans* because the benefit is set based on the employee's years of service and salary or seniority level. These traditional plans end at the death of the employee, unless it provides for the surviving spouse. In either event, the company needs to be notified of any deaths. If a death occurs mid-month, the company may require a refund of the remaining month's share payment.

Pension plans have been replaced with *defined contribution plans*, and include IRAs and employer-sponsored 401(k) plans. These accounts are funded directly from paychecks with pre-tax money and/or with separate contributions. After the age of 59.5 you can start taking out money without penalty. At age 70.5, you are required to take out money. When you die, and there is money in these accounts, they will go to the beneficiaries named in the plan administrator or with the financial institution. Beneficiaries of defined contribution plans are not named by will or trust.

K.   Next Steps to Creating Your Will

The next step to creating your will, after identifying the people and property in your will, is to identify other things that you should include in your will.

5. Identifying Other Things to Include with Your Will

Now that you have identified the people and property that you want to include in your will, next, you should identify some of the other things that you want to include with your will, including any powers of attorney. This will help your executor in the distribution of your estate and it will help you identify important things you want to pass on in your will or otherwise. This chapter covers things that do not fit within the people or property categories from the previous two chapters.

A. Estate Records Organizer

As you begin the process of gathering all of the information that your loved ones may need after you die, creating an estate records organizer can help get you organized. The estate records organizer can be a notebook or simply some pages put together with information ranging from your address, Social Security Number, e-mail usernames, to various passwords, and the locations of important documents. This information will help an executor, or anyone else, bring closure to your final arrangements. An estate records organizer is not required to be a part of your estate. You can leave the estate records organizer as part of your will or you can ask that the organizer only be given to the executor of the estate and then destroyed.

B.   Medical/End of Life Decisions

Your will is a legal document that will be read, and adhered to, upon your death. During a medical emergency, your will won't be consulted. Instead, physicians and hospitals will want to reference a separate document, called a living will, to determine what your emergency or end of life medical wishes are. State laws allow you to create a document which will serve as instructions to medical professionals about how you wish to be treated should you become unable to make these decisions yourself, for example, if you become incapacitated. State laws also allow you to name/appoint someone to make medical decisions for you if/when a situation occurs that you did not address in your living will through a document called a healthcare power of attorney.

Some states have combined the living will and healthcare power of attorney into a single document, usually called an *advanced healthcare directive*. No matter your state, you can create two separate documents. For the purposes of this book, the only difference is that your state may refer to the documents collectively or by two names.

The states that have combined the forms are: Alabama, Alaska, California, Delaware, Georgia, Hawaii, Idaho, Kentucky, Maine, Maryland, Minnesota, Mississippi, New Hampshire, New Mexico, North Dakota, Oklahoma, Oregon, Tennessee, Utah, Vermont, Virginia, and Wyoming.

Some states give you the option to combine the forms into a single document. The states are: Connecticut, Illinois, New Jersey, and South Carolina.

One of the primary benefits of making your   end of life healthcare decisions is to give yourself, and your loved ones, some peace of mind.

You get the peace of mind of knowing that your wishes regarding your healthcare are in writing and are available to your doctors and loved ones if they should ever need them. Many people who create these documents get a sense of self-relief from talking with their doctors, loved ones, and agents. If these documents are ever used, your loved ones will already be dealing with a lot.

Your loved ones will get some peace of mind too. Having these documents ready can take some of the burden off of their shoulders by not making them make difficult and very personal decisions that can leave them with deep feelings of guilt.

Creating your end of life healthcare documents is a sensible thing to do.

a)   Living Will

A *living will*, sometimes referred to as a *declaration to physicians* and as an *advanced healthcare directive*, is a legal document that instructs healthcare professionals on how they should treat you in the event that you are incapacitated. In other words, a living will controls whether or not you want to be on prolonged life support. Every state recognizes the living will.

In a living will, you state how you want your healthcare needs to be met. For example, you can dictate whether you want to be put on artificial life support or dictate that you prefer not to be resuscitated, sometimes referred to as a DNR (Do Not

Resuscitate). A living will keeps your family from making difficult decisions regarding your healthcare needs.

The living will is not the place to state your wishes regarding property transfer after you die or the place to explain why you are making the decisions that you making. If you want to provide any explanations about your decisions, include a separate document called an explanation letter. Also, a personal letter to loved ones to help them with your passing can be provided in a separate document called an ethical will. See the *Explanation Letters* and *Ethical Will* sections later in this chapter.

The living will only takes effect if you are not able to make your own decisions. Alzheimer's or forgetfulness will not be enough to justify the use of a living will. Being unable to make your own decisions means you are unconscious in some form. So long as you can make your own decisions, the living will does not have any legal effect. That means that so long as you are able to make your own decisions, you are free to change your mind without having to change your living will. If your wishes change, it is important to change your living will because if you are not able to make your own decisions, it will be difficult for anyone to contradict the living will.

Generally, two witnesses (three witnesses in Vermont) and a notary public are required to create a legally binding living will. The witnesses must be:

- at least 19 years of age, but a few states allow someone who is 18,
- of "sound mind" and able to understand the nature of the document they are signing,
- unaffiliated with your attending physician, the medical facility, or a patient of the attending physician or medical facility,

- someone not financially responsible for your healthcare costs,
- someone other than a beneficiary in your will or who has any claim to a portion of your estate upon your death, and
- unpaid.

In a few states, if you are in a hospital, nursing home, boarding facility, or other healthcare–type facility when you create the living will, a patient advocate, director of the facility, or patient ombudsman is required to be a third witness.

Every state allows you to revoke your living will. Witnesses are not required to revoke. States vary in what they require for revocation, but generally allow revocation by:

- destroying the living will by tearing it up, burning it, or some other physical act, but simply scratching through the signature will not be enough,
- creating a separate document that revokes the living will or instructions to a third party to destroy the living will at your direction,
- some states allow for an oral revocation, but only in the presence of witnesses who will sign and date a written revocation of the living will, or
- gestures by non-verbal or written statements are allowed in some states regardless of the person's physical or mental conditions.

b) Healthcare Power of Attorney

A *healthcare power of attorney*, sometimes called a *healthcare proxy*, gives another person the power to make your healthcare decisions.

A *power of attorney* is defined as giving another, your *agent* (also referred to as an *attorney-in-fact*), the legal right to make decisions on your behalf that you have not stated in other legal documents. It must be in writing.

The difference between the living will and the healthcare power of attorney is that in the living will you, yourself, state in advance how you want your healthcare situations to be handled if you become unable to do so, whereas the healthcare power of attorney gives that power to someone else, your agent. It is impossible to plan for every possible scenario. The healthcare power of attorney fills in the gaps.

The healthcare power of attorney is not the place to state your wishes regarding your healthcare. That is done in the living will. Also, you do not need to explain why you are making the decisions you are making. If you want to make any explanations, include an explanation letter. See the *Explanation Letters* section later in this chapter.

The healthcare power of attorney and the living will work together. What you want to do is create a living will to make the major decisions on the most common healthcare issues and then designate someone else to make the remaining decisions regarding your healthcare. The healthcare power of attorney takes effect when you become unable to make your own decisions. Therefore, you should choose someone trustworthy who knows and understands your wishes. It is important to be as clear as possible about your preferences because the court is reluctant to go against the decisions made by your power of attorney; these decisions include withholding medical care, medication, food, and even water.

Many married couples name their spouse (or partner) as their agent. The law does not interfere with this. If you become divorced, state law may have an effect on any healthcare power of attorney that was created during the marriage that names the former spouse as an agent. If you do become divorced, it is good practice to create a new healthcare power of attorney that names a new agent.

Some people may want to name multiple people as agents to share the decision making. This can be problematic due to the potential for conflict and disagreement. It is better to pick one person to serve as the agent and the other person to serve as the alternate agent.

States, generally, do not allow anyone that is involved in providing you with healthcare to be named as your agent. States are very strict on this matter. Even if there is no cloud of dishonesty, states presume one exists by the nature of the relationship. For that reason you should avoid naming anyone that will be, or is likely to be, involved in providing you with your healthcare needs. This includes physicians, nurses, aides, technicians, as well as any administrative persons.

You should talk with your agent and your alternate agent about your wishes. The more they know about your wishes, the more likely your wishes will be followed. The powers you give to your agent are deeply personal. Emotions can run deep.

With healthcare power of attorney forms, your agent will have access to your records as your personal representative under the *Health Insurance Portability and Accountability Act* (*HIPAA*).

Your primary physician will play an important role. They may be required to physically examine you under your healthcare power of attorney. You should discuss candidly with your primary physician about your wishes. You should also talk with any alternate doctors (if any). It is good practice to let them know you have created the healthcare power of attorney. You may even want to give them a copy so they have it.

Much like creating a will, to create a healthcare power of attorney, you must be of legal age and of "sound mind."

The legal age is usually 18 years old (except in Alabama you must be 19, and in Nebraska you must be 19 or married).

A "sound mind" is the ability to understand what the document means and how it will work at the time the document is created. If you are physically disabled and cannot sign your own name, but are of legal age and of "sound mind," you can enter into a healthcare power of attorney by making your mark (an "X" is acceptable) and directing another to sign their name with a statement that explains that the document was signed at the creator's direction. For example, A is unable to sign her name, but wants to create a power of attorney. A asks B to sign his name. A makes an "X" and B signs B's name and writes a statement "B is signing this power of attorney at the direction of A who cannot sign A's name, but has made their mark, is of "sound mind," and of legal age."

If someone signs their name in place of yours, make sure that they sign their own name and not your name. Signing someone else's name is forgery and is a crime.

In general, the same rules and laws regarding witnesses and revocation that apply to living wills also apply to the healthcare power of attorney. You should also name an alternate.

In the event that you do not create a healthcare power of attorney, doctors will look to state laws. In some states, doctors are required to consult with your spouse, partner, or immediate relatives.

There are special considerations for pregnant women. Your state may or may not honor your wishes, depending on the state's laws and the trimester you are in.

The Supreme Court of the United States has said that your right to direct your own healthcare matters is guaranteed by the U.S. Constitution. States cannot violate the U.S. Constitution, however, States can, and do, put restrictions on certain healthcare situations.

In addition to federal and state laws, another consideration is that your hospital may not honor all of your healthcare wishes. For example, some hospitals are religious based or affiliated hospitals and their polices and procedures may contradict your wishes. Catholic hospitals are part of the U.S. Conference of Catholic Bishops and require that all patients receive food and water. Even if you have a healthcare power of attorney that contradicts this policy, the Catholic hospital will follow its own policy.

If you have wishes that may contradict a hospital's policy, you should plan ahead for where you should go in case of an emergency.

c) Organ, Tissue, and Body Donation

After you die, your loved ones and/or executor will be asked whether you wanted to donate your organs, or other body parts, for medical or scientific purposes. The recipient of the organs pays the expenses and not the donor's family. There are many reasons why a person would want, or not want, to donate their organs, tissue, and/or body such as for religious reasons. Whatever your personal reasons are, you should make your wishes clear to your loved ones and executor.

Your organs can be used to save someone else's life. Your organs may be used for teaching medical students or for medical research and/or experimentation.

You can donate organs and tissue including your heart, liver, kidneys, pancreas, eyes (corneas), lungs, skin, and various tendons for transplant.

If you plan on donating your body to science, it may go to a university. Generally, once the university is done with your body, it will be cremated and your ashes will be scattered in a designated plot of land. You can also make other arrangements. Remember that just because you want your body to go to science does not mean that it will be accepted and therefore you should make alternative arrangements.

You can choose to donate just organs, just tissue, or your entire body. You can be as specific as you want to be about which specific organs and/or tissue you would, or would not, like to donate.

C. Financial Durable Power of Attorney

Much like the healthcare power of attorney, the *financial durable power of attorney* allows you to appoint someone to handle your financial matters in the event that you are unable to make your own decisions. The financial durable power of attorney will not take effect unless, or until, you are physically unable to make your own decisions. A financial durable power of attorney does not grant the power to make healthcare decisions; you will need to create a healthcare power of attorney for that.

The requirements for selecting your agent are the same requirements for creating your will. Your agent must be of legal age and of "sound mind." The legal age is generally 18 (except in Alabama you must be at least 19 and in Nebraska you must be at least 19 or married). You can also appoint more than one agent, but this is generally not advised because there is an increased possibility of conflicts between co-agents. These are also the same requirement for who can create a financial power of attorney.

Generally, if you are married, you would want to name your spouse, unless your spouse is mentally or physically unable to do the task or there is the potential for conflict. Your spouse may not necessarily be the best person to be your agent. Your spouse already likely has the authority to pay normal bills through a joint bank account using their own name, but the spouse may run into problems if the spouse needs to sell assets that are owned by both spouses. For example, most states require consent from both spouses to sell real estate. It may be easier to name a third party as your agent. Your spouse will retain their right to joint accounts.

The person you name as your agent will have the power to sign documents on your behalf, saying that they have your permission to sign their name in place of yours. The power remains in effect even if you become mentally insane, disabled, or incompetent.

It is important to name someone that you not only trust, but who is good with money. You can limit the person's power in the way you feel is best. For example, you may not want the person to sell your car or house, or to not go into debt over a certain amount.

To be effective, your agent is going to need information to perform their tasks. You should provide them as much detail as you can to help them serve your best interests.

You can grant the power to:

- pay your bills, expenses, and taxes,
- collect and file for Social Security, Medicare, or other government programs,
- operate your small business,
- hire someone to represent you in court,
- make gifts or transfer your property into an already existing trust, and/or
- make banking transactions and retirement decisions.

With these powers, your assets will be vulnerable to bad acts committed by the agent. Even family members who want to contradict your agent will find it challenging to go against the agent. State laws require agents to be prudent (not lose money), but do allow agents to make ordinary transactions for the benefit of the estate. Reasonable transactions will generally not be contradicted by the court simply because in hindsight the transaction turned out to lose money.

Gifts over a certain amount ($13,000 as of the date of this book) in a calendar year will require the filing of a federal gift tax return. Gifts to spouses are not taxed. Also, gifts to pay medical expenses, tuition, and gifts to tax-exempt charities (501(c)(3)s) are not subject to a gift tax under certain circumstances.

State laws require agents to keep detailed records. The records must record every transaction that takes place. The general requirement is enough of a record for the agent to show where and how money has been transacted. The agent may need to file tax returns and send out expense records to family members.

The agent's power ends when you die, the court invalidates the power (extremely rare), or when you revoke the power, which you can do so long as you are of "sound mind."

Your agent will have broad powers of your finances. One financial area that your agent will not have power over is any living trusts. The property must be in the living trust at the time the power of attorney takes effect for this to apply.

Often a family member may consider forgery. It is commonly self-justified because you are using their money to pay their bills. No problem, right? The problem is that it is textbook forgery. It is a crime in every state. Just because charges are not brought forward (although they might be), does not mean there are no negative consequences. It is a common enough practice that a judge will pick-up on. A judge who discovers, or reasonably suspects forgery (because there is no financial durable power of attorney, but all bills are being paid), even in the smallest instance, may not be so quick to give control over to a relative who has proven themselves to be a liar. The reason is to protect against family members who loot relative's of assets. The best practice is to not do it.

You should name an alternate agent. If your agent resigns then the alternate will takes over. If the alternate resigns, or no alternate is named, then if you allow it, then the agent can name another to act as your agent. This power is known as a *delegation*.

To create your power of attorney, you must sign in front of a notary public. In addition, a few state require witnesses. Arizona (one witness), California (two witnesses or notarized), Connecticut (two witnesses), Delaware (one witness), Washington, D.C. (two witnesses, but only required if the power of attorney is to be recorded), Florida (two witness), Georgia (two witnesses), Illinois (one witness), Maryland (two witnesses), Michigan (two witnesses, but only required if the power of attorney is to be recorded), New York (two witnesses, but only required if completing the Statutory Gifts Rider, see note below), Oklahoma (two witnesses), Pennsylvania (two witnesses, but only required if the power of attorney is marked and not signed or if signed by another person at your direction), South Carolina (two witnesses), and Vermont (one witness).

Most states do not require a written acknowledgement from the agent. The states that require it are: California, Georgia, Montana, New Hampshire, New York, Pennsylvania, and Vermont.

To revoke, you must be of "sound mind." This is the same standard required to create the power of attorney. If you can understand the concept of revoking your document then you are likely of "sound mind." You can revoke either by preparing a separate document, by physically destroying all of the copies of the document, or both. Once you have revoked the document, you must notify all those that have received or have likely received the document and relied on it (e.g., banks, Social Security office, insurance companies, etc.). If you revoke your power of attorney, but fail to notify a third party that has reasonably relied on it, then they may be able to prevail against your estate for the full amount. The reason is to provide reliability and use of a power of attorney. Once a notice has been given, then third parties can no longer rely on the power of attorney.

Most states do not require the recording of a power of attorney unless real estate transactions are involved. The exceptions are North Carolina (the power of attorney must be filed within 30 days at the Register of Deeds) and South Carolina (a copy of the power of attorney must be filed in the county records or land registry office). If you want to record in Illinois, Kentucky, or

Minnesota you will need to include a list of the names and addresses of people who prepared the forms. In most states, the power of attorney is recorded in the same office that real estate is recorded.

**New York requires any agent who makes significant transfers of property on behalf of the estate to include an additional form with the financial durable power of attorney called a New York Statutory Gift Rider form. The form must be signed in front of a notary public and two witnesses. It is required when the agent is given the power to:

- transfer property into your living trust,
- make changes to a title of a bank account held jointly with someone other than the agent,
- make changes to pay-on-death (POD/Totten trust) bank accounts,
- make changes to life insurance or retirement beneficiaries,
- use the power of attorney for any personal benefit of the agent,
- mix property with agent's property, or

make gifts over $500.**

D. Limited Minor Child Care Power of Attorney

A *limited minor child care power of attorney* gives someone other than the legal guardians the power to make decisions regarding a minor child concerning medical care, school enrollment, and/or act as guardian if the legal guardians become incapacitated. A minor child is anyone under the age of 18. Only legal guardians, such as parents or adopted parents, can enter into a limited minor child power of attorney.

The powers of the agent are limited to those that are granted in the document. If there is no mention of the power, or the power is not initialed next to, then the power is not granted. The powers granted in this document cannot be used to release a minor for adoption or consent to adoption or marriage.

The power of attorney cannot contain an automatic renewal clause. You would need to create a new power of attorney to renew.

Even where in place, the powers of the legal guardians are not limited by those of the agent. The agent cannot contradict the legal guardians.

The reason why legal guardians would want to enter into this type of a power of attorney is to give another person permission to make decisions regarding minor children because the legal guardians may not be available at the time. It is ideal for legal guardians who are planning a trip. Even when going on a short trip, legal guardians may want to create this document, especially regarding healthcare for a minor child.

A limited minor child care power of attorney is distinguishable from a limited guardianship, which is where the legal guardians, who are still alive, voluntarily give temporary parental responsibilities to another. Where entered into, the legal guardians temporarily lose parental making responsibilities. Formal proceedings in a probate or family court are required. The limited minor child care power of attorney cannot be used for this purpose.

A limited minor child care power of attorney is distinguishable from a guardianship, which is created in probate court after the death of the minor child's legal guardians. Parents appoint guardians for minor children in their will (or other signed, witnessed, and notarized documents) or the court will appoint someone. The limited minor child care power of attorney cannot be used for this purpose.

E.   Trusts

A trust is an abstract idea and requires some "legal fiction" meaning there is nothing that can be touched or seen, but does exist as far as the law is concerned. A *trust* is defined as the placing of confidence in a person, called a *trustee*, for the purpose of making the trustee the owner of property, to hold or use the property for the benefit of one or more other people, as directed by the creator of the trust. Once your trust is created, the trustee, not you, are the legal owners of the property in the trust. You can name multiple trustees to the same or different trusts.

Your agent of a durable financial power of attorney does not have any authority over trust property. The agent will not be able to create, modify, or revoke a trust on your behalf.

You can create a trust in your lifetime that names you as the trustee and the property is distributed after you die (called a *living trust*). Also, a trust can be created after you die under instructions that you leave in a will or elsewhere. Trust property is managed by the trustee. A trust is preferred by those looking to avoid probate and privacy because a trust does not become part of the public record, unless approved by a court or trustee. Probate records become part of the public record.

A living trust can serve as a substitute for a will if all of the property is named in the living trust. Even if you create a living trust (not included in this book) you should create a will to cover any potential gaps as it is difficult to place everything into a living trust. A trust is not right for everyone or every situation.

For people with relatively modest estates, a will can meet all of their needs.

Placing property into a living trust does not shield the property from calculations of government benefits such as Medicare and Social Security benefits.

F.   Social Security

When you die if you have worked long enough as specified by the Social Security Administration (SSA), your family may get some benefits. To get Social Security benefit, you, as well as the family member to receive the benefits, must qualify. Social Security benefits are determined by the SSA. You should have the paperwork. Your family or executor will need to file the appropriate papers.

Some of the benefits that your family may receive are a $225 one time lump sum payment and monthly paid benefits.

A $225 one time lump sum is paid, in order of priority, to the surviving spouse, and if there is no surviving spouse, then the lump sum will be paid to a child who is eligible for benefits on your record in the month of your death.

The surviving spouse is eligible if:

- you both were living together at the time of your death, or
- if you were living apart, the surviving spouse can still collect if the surviving spouse was receiving certain Social Security benefits (because of its complexity, this topic is beyond the scope of this book; seek additional resources by contacting the SSA or an attorney).

Monthly paid benefits to your widow or widower, unmarried children, or a few others who may qualify. Payments may be made to:

- a widow or widower who is:
    - age 60 or older (age 50 or older if disabled),
    - at any age, but is caring for any of your (the deceased) surviving children under age 16, or
    - at any age, but is caring for any of your (the deceased) surviving children who are disabled.
- an unmarried child of yours (the deceased) who is:
    - under 18 years of age (or up to age 19 if the unmarried child is a full-time student in an elementary or secondary school), or
    - over 18 years of age and has disability that began before they were 22 years of age
- your (the deceased) stepchild, grandchild, step-grandchild, or adopted child under certain circumstances (because of its complexity this topic is beyond the scope of this book; seek additional resources by contacting the SSA or an attorney),
- your (the deceased) parents, age 62 or older, who were dependent on you for at least half of their support, or
- your (the deceased) surviving, divorced spouse if they:
    - are 62 years of age or older,
    - were married to you for at least 10 years,
    - have been divorced for two or more years,
    - unmarried, and
    - are not by themselves, or with someone else, eligible for equal or greater Social Security benefits.

To find out if you qualify for Social Security benefits you should contact the SSA toll-free at 1-800-772-1213 (for the deaf or hard of hearing, call TTY number, 1-800-325-0778) between 7a.m. to 7p.m. Monday-Friday. Calling the SSA allows you to plan, as well as, ensure that your family gets the benefits you have worked for during your lifetime.

When you die, the SSA must be notified as soon as possible to start the process. Generally, the funeral director does this for you, and will need your Social Security number. If the funeral director does not do this, then the executor or any family member can make the report.

Once the SSA process has started, the SSA will need:

- a certified copy of your death certificate,
- a copy of your marriage certificate,
- the Social Security numbers of:
    - you,
    - the surviving spouse, and the divorced spouse in certain circumstances,
    - any of your surviving unmarried children under the age of 18 (19 if the unmarried child is a full-time student in an elementary or secondary school), or any unmarried child of yours who has a disability that began before they were 22 years of age,
    - stepchild, grandchild, step-grandchild, or adopted child under certain circumstances, and/or
    - your parents who are older than 62 and who were dependent on you for at least half of their support.
- tax returns and W-2s for the past two years and information about your employer for the past two years.

G. Death Certificates

A death certificate is legal proof that someone has died. A death certificate is required for various things including life, car, and homeowner's insurance policies, bank accounts, stocks, bonds, and mutual funds. The government uses them to stop Social Security payments and other benefits.

Death certificates are, generally, closed from general public records for a period of time, usually 25 to 50 years. You cannot just go to the local health department and get a copy of a person's death certificate without some reason or relationship to the deceased. This is to protect private information. Therefore, getting a death certificate requires specific information.

States differ as to what information is required to obtain a death certificate. However, states request most of the same information. The death certificate is usually handled by the funeral director in the place where you are buried or cremated.

The information requested includes basic information such as name, address, and Social Security number, but can include race, diseases, and level of education.

The executor of your estate should get about 20 copies of the death certificate, but may need more depending on your estate.

H. Self-Proving Affidavits

A *self-proving affidavit* is as a document that affirms that your will was signed by you in the presences of the witnesses and the notary public who all, together, watched you sign the will and that you knew you were signing for the purpose of creating your will. The purpose of the self-proving affidavits is to allow the will to be admitted into probate court without needing to contact the witnesses to prove the authenticity of the will.

The notary public puts their mark on a separate paper that is attached to the will. Note: the notary public is not making any statements about the will itself and is not notarizing the will. The separate sheet of paper is needed as the notary public is notarizing only the self-proving affidavits that states that the will was signed and witnessed by two people. This distinction is important. A notary may be reluctant to notarize a will, which is not the same as notarizing the self-proving affidavits.

A Notary Public may have their own form that they use for a self-proving affidavit. You can use either form, but often a notary public will not have their own form for self-proving affidavits. In that case, you will need to provide a form.

A will can be entered into probate without a self-proving affidavit. Without self-proving affidavits, the court will likely first make a determination about the authenticity of the will. This may mean calling the witnesses to testify. The self-proving affidavit makes the process easier.

State laws are not uniform in regard to what is required in self-proving affidavits. California treats the witness signatures as the self-proving affidavit and no separate affidavit is needed. New Hampshire does allow the use of self-proving affidavits but requires special language that is beyond the scope of this book. If you want a self-proving affidavit in New Hampshire you will need to consult a licensed lawyer in your area. Louisiana, Washington, D.C., Maryland, Ohio and Vermont do not recognize them. The rest do.

I.   Ethical Will

An *ethical will* has no legal effect because it is not a will, but is rather a statement you make in writing that your executor passes on to loved ones. It is sometimes called a *legacy letter*.

The ethical will can be in the form of a:

- letter, a sentence, or any other statement you wish to make,
- diary or journal that you have kept over time,
- video so your loved ones can see and hear your voice, or
- special care package you leave for each of your loved ones.

You can have the executor keep the contents of the documents private so only the beneficiary that the ethical will is addressed to knows what is inside. You can choose how and what you want to say. The idea is to say something you:

- thought you would have the rest of your life to say,
- were unable or afraid to say during your lifetime,
- to help your loved ones cope with your passing,
- explain the process of what will happen now that you have died, and
- want to pass on such as knowledge and advice you have gained over the years.

J.   Explanation Letters

An *explanation letter* can help resolve disputes. Because your will does not generally provide information about why you distributed your property in the way that you did, the explanation letter can help fill that gap.

The explanation letter can detail what you hope your beneficiaries will do with your property once you pass. While it has no legal effect, the explanation letter may be used in court where there is a dispute.

The explanation letter can be combined with your ethical will to provide some closure and understanding of your last wishes.

K.   Inform the World of Your Death

One of the jobs of the executor will be to inform the world that you have died. Your executor should have ready access to the people you want to be contacted, along with any message you want to leave them.

Also, you will want to create a biographical information sheet about yourself. This sheet should include things like where you were born, what you enjoyed about life, and any special people, places, and memories you have. You may want to include information about who your parents, grandparents, and other relatives were to pass on that knowledge to the next generation.

When your executor informs the world of your death, the biographical information you put together should help your executor inform the world about your life. This section focuses on how your executor will go about informing the world of your death, based on the information you leave behind.

a)   Funeral, Cremation, and Memorial Services

Most people pay for their funeral, cremation, and memorial services on their own, by either purchasing an insurance policy, or paying for the arrangements ahead of time. If you do this, then you need to leave a copy of your contract and other information for the executor about these arrangements.

The difference between a funeral service and a memorial service is that at a funeral service the body is present whereas with a memorial service the body is not because it has been cremated or is otherwise unavailable. After the funeral service, the body is buried. Cremation is the burning of the body and the scattering of the ashes in accordance with your wishes, either over a grave or in some body of water like a river.

Issues you may wish to address:

- who should attend, including family, friends, and religious clergy,
- where and what time of day you want the ceremony,
- gravestone inscription,
- flowers to mark your grave,
- your preference for burial or cremation, and should be open or closed casket,
- any pallbearers,
- transportation to the grave and if you want a graveside ceremony,
- reception afterwards to celebrate your life, or
- any special requests such as a last song or prayer.

b) Newspaper Obituary Information

Newspapers and a few other publications print obituaries. You may wish to have your obituary published in your local newspaper or a larger publication. You may want to write your own obituary. If you don't want to draft the full version, you can draft an outline of things you want said or not said.

An obituary normally includes:

- a picture,
- your full name,
- place and date of birth and death,
- place, date, and time of any service held in your honor, as well as whoever is invited,

- who survives you,
- where you will be buried or where your ashes will be scattered,
- details about your life accomplishments,
- awards,
- education,
- military service,
- membership and activity in the community or religious organizations,
- where people can send flowers and gifts,
- hobbies, or
- any other message or statement you wish to make.

L.   Next Steps to Creating Your Will

Before you start to create your will, you need to get organized. If you have all of the information you need in front of you, you will spend less time creating your will. Then begin creating your will.

III. Trusts

1. Introduction to Creating Your Own Trust

One of the fastest ways to transfer property after your death is through a living trust because trusts are not required to go through probate court. In addition to avoiding probate costs, a trust lets you control who will receive property after you die. This section provides information you need to create your own trust.

To create a trust you do not always need a lawyer, especially for simple living trusts. All you really need is a little bit of intelligence and the right information.

If you do decide to retain a lawyer after looking through this book, then this book can still provide valuable information to help keep you informed as to what your lawyer is doing regarding your property.

Before you actually start filling out a living trust form, it is important to understand some basic information about the functions and uses of trusts. Then you can start to identify the property you want to put into your living trust and the people who you want to name as beneficiaries and trustees.

Planning your trust before you begin can help you to think about what are some of the things a trust can and cannot do for your estate. To make a trust you will need to educate yourself on the options you have when creating your trust.

The following chart shows the steps to create your own living trust. This book is organized in this layout.

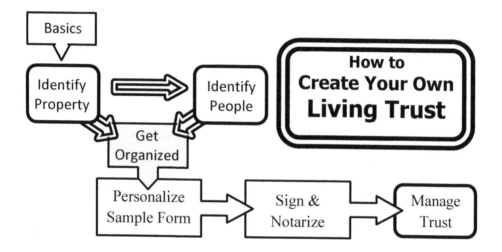

2. Basics—Functions and Uses of Trusts

The first step to creating your trust is to understand what a trust is and why you are creating it. This chapter takes you through the basics of trusts. Along with explaining the basic functions of a trust, this chapter will help you determine what type of trust you need, and what, if any, additional resources you might need.

A. What Is a Trust?

A trust is an abstract idea and requires some "legal fiction" meaning there is nothing that can be touched or seen, but does exist as far as the law is concerned. A *trust* is defined as the placing of confidence in a person, called a *trustee*, for the purpose of making the trustee the owner of property, to hold or use the property for the benefit of one or more other people, as directed by the creator of the trust. Once your trust is created, the trustee, not you, are the legal owners of the property in the trust. You can name multiple trustees to the same or different trusts.

You can create a trust in your lifetime that names you as the trustee and the property is distributed after you die (called a *living trust*). Also, a trust can be created after you die under instructions that you leave in a will or elsewhere. Trust property is managed by the trustee. A trust is preferred by those looking to avoid probate and privacy because a trust does not become part of the public record, unless approved by a court or trustee. Probate records become part of the public record.

A living trust can serve as a substitute for a will if all of the property is named in the living trust. Even if you create a living trust, you should create a will to cover any potential gaps as it is difficult to place everything into a living trust.

Agent of a durable financial power of attorney do not have any authority over trust property. The agent will not be able to create, modify, or revoke a trust on your behalf.

Placing property into a living trust does not shield the property from calculations of government benefits such as Medicare and Social Security benefits.

B.   Who Can Create a Trust?

The person who is the creator of the trust is referred to as the *settlor, grantor,* or *trustor.* The settlor exercises no control over the property after the trust is created and a list of rules governing how the property in the trust is to be managed and distributed will guide the trustee to carry out the settlor's wishes.

A settlor must be at least 18 years of age and have the rights to ownership in the property. The property can be shared with another person. If the property that is put into trust is shared, then only the settlor's share of the property can be put into the trust and no more because the settlor cannot give more than the settlor owns.

C.   What Does a Trust Require?

A trust requires that you put property into it and that you name beneficiaries to receive the property. The type of property that you can put into the trust, your marital status, and when the trust will be created will determine what type of trust you need. Putting property in trust means the completion of documents that name the property to be transferred into the trust. The document must make a declaration to place the property in the trust of the trustee for the purposes laid out in the document. The date the property is transferred can be either the date of completing the documents that create the trust or at a later date, such as on your death.

The documents to create a trust must be:

- signed by the creator(s) who is/are of "sound mind" at the time of signing, and
- notarized.

Witnesses are only required in Florida.

A "sound mind" requires that, at the time that you *execute* the living trust (i.e., when you sign and date your living trust in front of a notary public), you:

- know what a living trust is, what it does, and that you are creating a living trust,
- name trust beneficiaries that have a relationship to you that you understand, and
- you understand the nature and extent of your property that is included in your living trust.

If you can understand the concept of a "sound mind," you are probably of "sound mind."

In general, a trustee must also be named, but some jurisdictions allow a trustee to be named later. It is best practice to name a trustee in your trust.

If the trust property will go to minor children (anyone under the age of 18), a guardian must be named to look after the property left in trust for the minor children.

Unlike a will that is only valid after a probate judge approves the will, a trust is not required to go through probate court and the living trust is valid in your lifetime (hence the name, "living trust.") The reason is the because when you create a trust, you are no longer the legal owner of the property in the trust, the trustee is the owner of the property.

D. What a Trust Can Do for Your Estate

Avoid probate. The property that is placed into the trust avoids probate because when the trust is created, the trustee is the lawful owner off the property in the trust, not you.

Reduce estate taxes. If used correctly, a trust can be used to reduce estate taxes. However, this really only applies to really large estates. As of 2013, that would mean estates greater than $5.35 million.

Provide for your minor child(ren). A trust can be used to provide for you minor child(ren) by providing them with trust property for medical, education, and living expenses. A trust for minor child(ren) will also manage the property in the trust for the child(ren) until they reach the age of majority (usually 18) or the age specified in the terms of the trust.

Quickly distribute property. Probate can take months and in some cases, years. A trust can quickly distribute trust property to the named beneficiaries after your death because it does not require court approval before distributing it.

Keep property distribution of property private. A trust can allow you to keep the property you keep in the trust and its distribution private because the trust does not need court approval, there is no disclosure requirement to anyone other than the government. However, many states require disclosure to family members of all trusts created and distributed by your estate.

Provide an alternative to creating a will. Creating a trust can also be used as an alternative to creating a will by naming all of your property in a trust. If you have no property left over, then there is no need for a will. We recommend you create both, a will and a trust.

E. What a Trust Cannot Do for Your Estate

Eliminate estate taxes. Estate taxes can be reduced or delayed, but a trust property that is disturbed is still subject to taxes. There is always a taxpayer.

Keep distributions completely private. Most states require the trust be disclosed to family members. Also, real estate transfers must be recorded in public records. Any lawsuits involving the trust will be made public.

Cut family completely out of your estate. A trust, like a will, can be contested by your heirs. Although a trust does not go through probate, an heir who wants to contest a trust you have left to another heir can do so under the same theory of law as they could under a will. Most states require disclosure to family members.

F. What Is the Difference Between a Trust and a Will?

There are many kinds of wills. But, in short, a *will* is a written document that controls how your property will be disturbed when you die, who will serve as guardians of your minor children (and who will take care of the minor children's property until they reach 18), and how your property will be managed upon your death. The person whose property is affected by the will is called the *testator*. If it is your will, you are the testator.

One of the primary advantages of creating a will is that you control how your property will be distributed when you die and/or how your children will be taken care of. However, a will is only valid once a court (usually a probate court) approves the will. A trust, on the other hand, does not need to go through the court system to be valid. Once created, a trust is valid. A trust avoid probate. Neither a will or trust can really be used to avoid taxes all together as, generally there is a tax payer. A trust can help you distribute your property over a period of time and that can help to reduce your tax burden.

Trusts, unlike wills, do not become part of the public record. Any transfers into a trust can be kept private from family members, but are not kept private from the IRS.

G. How to Change an Existing Trust

An existing trust may not always be changed depending on what type of trust has been created.

Living trust. A living trust can be changed because it is a trust you create while you are still alive and add property to it during your lifetime. You can remove property as you want by making changes to trust Schedule or codicil. The changes made by codicil should be minor changes.

Totten trust. A Totten trust can be changed because you are free to add or remove money from the bank account. By closing or removing all of the money you can change it. You can also change who you name as the beneficiary. There is no requirement to inform a beneficiary that they have been named as a beneficiary.

Minor child(ren)'s trust. A child(ren)'s trust once it has been created is very difficult to change by the person who created it because the trust then is owned by the trustees until the child (ren) reach the age specified by the trust.

H. Types of Trusts

There are many types of trusts. Below are a few examples of trusts that you can create instead of, or along with, your will.

a) Testamentary Trust

A *testamentary trust*, sometimes called a *will trust*, is a trust that you create in your will by stating that on your death, the trust is to be created. It cannot be created until after your death. The testamentary trust is created by your trustee or the person appointed by a probate court to handle your final arrangements. These trusts protect against creditors, reduce taxes, and allow you to have some control over how your property will be disturbed upon your death.

b) Living Trust

A *living trust* is a trust where the creator of the trust acts as the trustee of their own trust until their death, when the property is distributed according to the terms set out in the trust. The living trust is also called an *inter-vivos* or *revocable trust*. The creator of the trust can change and destroy the trust prior to their death, but, after their death, the trust is irrevocable. The trust does not go through probate and passes automatically to the named beneficiaries. You need to name an alternate trustee to manage the trust after you die. The main disadvantage of creating this type of trust, instead of a will, is that the trust requires a lot of management. The only property that will be subject to the trust is property that you specifically designate to the trust. Any property that you do not specifically put in the trust will pass according to your will or by state law.

i. Individual Living Trust

If you are unmarried, you can use a living trust to leave all or part of your property to the named beneficiaries. You can also use it to create a trust for any minor child(ren) you may have.

If you are married, you can use the individual living trust if you most of your property is owned individually. This is especially true for newly married couples.

ii.   Married Living Trust

Married couples have special considerations because the property that they owned is generally owned together. Both spouses can agree to leave all other their property to the other who survives them and then after the surviving spouse's death to the named beneficiary. Both the husband and wife are the creators of the trust and are also the trustees. You can also use it to create a trust for any minor child(ren).

1.   Simple Married Living Trust

For most married couples, the simple married living makes the most sense. Each member of the couple acts as a co-grantor and co-trustee of the trust. However, each person may choose any beneficiary they may desire for their share of commonly owned property and for individually owned property in the trust. Both will have control over all of the property in the trust. Either person may revoke the trust at any time. If that happens, the ownership of the property returns to where it was before the trust was created.

When one of the spouses dies, the property originally contributed by that spouse will be distributed. Any property distributed to the surviving spouse will remain in the trust. The trust then continues until the death of the second spouse. The surviving spouse will then own all of the trust property and can distribute to the beneficiaries they wish regardless of which spouse brought the property into the trust originally.

2.   AB Living Trust

If you want to make sure that each spouse's property goes to their separate beneficiaries regardless of which spouse dies first, an AB living trust may be a better choice than a married living trust or a simple will. One of the primary reasons you would want to create an AB living trust is because it keeps the estate of the deceased spouse legally separate from the estate of the surviving spouse, while allowing the surviving spouse to benefit from the deceased spouse's property. This can be crucial for combined estates that are over the estate tax threshold.

With an *AB living trust*, or sometimes called an *exemption* or *bypass* trust, the property contributed to the trust by the first spouse to die will be distributed to the first spouse's beneficiaries after the death of the surviving spouse. The surviving spouse cannot change the beneficiaries of the deceased spouse's trust property. The surviving spouse will retain control and enjoyment of the property for their lifetime.

In this trust, both spouse list out their separate property and their beneficiaries. They also name the property that is shared. This meets the legal requirement that the property be separated. Upon the death of the first spouse, their separate property is put into trust A and the surviving spouse's property is put into trust B. The surviving spouse still retains full use of all property in both trusts. Upon the death of the surviving spouse, both trusts are distributed according to the named beneficiaries.

3. AB Disclaimer Living Trust

The AB disclaimer living trust is very similar to the AB living trust except in the *AB disclaimer living trust*, rather than requiring that upon the first spouse's death, trust B be created and requiring that it be funded with all or a portion of the deceased spouse's estate under a marital deduction formula, the disclaimer trust leaves the decision as to whether to create such a trust until the death of the first spouse because the surviving spouse may not need the marital deduction tax advantage.

c) Marital Trust

A *marital trust*, also called a *marital deduction trust* or an *"A" trust*, is created to take advantage of the Federal marital deduction which allows one spouse to transfer all of their property to the other spouse, in their lifetime, without being taxed. After death, transfers to the surviving spouse are subject to estate taxes. To qualify for the marital deduction, only the surviving spouse can be the beneficiary of the trust and must have the right to receive income from the trust during his or her lifetime. No matter how valuable the property in the trust is, even if it exceeds that year's Federal estate tax exemption amount, your spouse won't owe any Federal estate taxes on that property. The surviving spouse does not necessarily have to take distributions of income unless required to do so by the terms of the trust. Since the trust property were not taxed at the first spouse's death, whatever remains in the trust at the death of the surviving spouse is subject to taxation in that spouse's estate. Only after your death, will your spouse has the right to use the property in the trust. The surviving spouse only gets a general power of appointment to allow the surviving spouse to control the ultimate distribution of the trust property and to modify the way property are distributed at his or her death, if your spouse so chooses.

d) Totten Trust

A *Totten trust*, also called a *Payable on Death (POD) account*, is where one person adds money to a bank account that designates that whatever is in the account when they die, will be passed on to the named beneficiary. You can revoke the account at any time until your death or close the account. The bank account can be used as you normal do. To create a Totten trust you only need to complete a form with your bank. The form is retained by your bank and you will get a copy as well. The beneficiary does not need to be informed or give consent for you to name them as a beneficiary. At the death of the creator of the Totten trust, the funds automatically become the property of the named beneficiary.

e) Child(ren)'s Trust

A *child(ren)'s trust* is a trust created for child(ren), generally, by parents, to be managed by an adult until the child(ren) reach a certain age. The age can be any age you choose such as 25 or 40. This trust is created for the benefit of minor child(ren) who, at the age of 18, would no longer be under the care of a guardian, but their parents/creators think it is in the child(ren)'s best interest to have the trust property managed beyond the child (ren)'s 18th birthday. You can name the same person as both the guardian of your child(ren) and as the trustee of your child (ren)'s trust. You do not have to name your surviving spouse. You should also name an alternate trustee.

You may also choose to name a property guardian for the property you leave to your minor child(ren). Property guardians are required to report to the court, about the property they manage, on a regular basis. Property guardian's authority to manage the property is governed/limited by state laws. The property guardian must turn over all property to the child when that child reaches the age of majority (usually 18).

The trustee is authorized to spend up to the amount in the trust for the well-being of the child(ren), including medical expenses, education, and maintenance. The trustee is responsible for investing trust property, paying taxes on behalf of the child(ren), and using the trust property to meet the child(ren)'s needs. The court is generally not involved in the trustee's decision making.

3. Identifying the Property and People in Your Trust

Once you understand the basic functions of a trust, your next step is to understand the property and people you can name as part of your trust. In this chapter, you will learn about the different property and people in your trust.

A. Property

Unlike the will where you would want to think about the people first, in a trust it makes more sense to start by thinking about what property that you want to put into your trust because the trust does not need to contain all of the property in your estate.

a) Real Estate

You can transfer real estate into a living trust to avoid probate. If you own the real estate as joint tenants or tenancy by the entirety you are already avoid probate so it may not make sense to create a living trust with your real estate in it. One of the other reasons to leave real estate in a living trust where there are joint owners (but not with a joint tenancy because of the rights of survivorship) is to provide for who will receive the real estate in the event that both owners die at the same time.

You can put real estate in an AB trust or AB disclaimer trust and potentially reduce tax liability because the real estate will be legally separate from the property of the surviving spouse.

If you do place real estate into a living trust, you do not need to notify your insurance company including your home owner's insurance, or the IRS because you are still the owner of the house during your lifetime.

b) Non-Real Estate

You can put into the trust almost any non-real estate property into your living trust that is legally owned by you. You must own some share of the property, but do not have to be in actual possession of the property.

Stocks and other securities. Stocks and other securities can be transferred into a living trust. Most brokerage accounts are familiar with living trusts to make the transfer. Once into the trust, all of the stocks and dividends are owned by the trust and you are the trustee so you will retain control. But, individual stock certificates will require you to get certificates issued in the trust's name. U.S. treasury bills can be placed into a living trust.

Money market accounts and bank accounts. You can put money market accounts and bank accounts into either a Totten trust or into a living will. A Totten trust does not usually allow you to name alternate beneficiaries. If you name more than one beneficiary in a Totten trust and one of your beneficiaries dies, then the remaining beneficiaries will split the amount in the trust with nothing going to the deceased or the deceased's estate.

Copyrights, patents, and royalties. You can transfer your right to any copyrights, patents, and future royalties you own into a living trust.

Minerals, oil, and gas interests. These are more complicated and you should seek the advice of a licensed attorney on adding these to your living trust.

c) Property That Should Not Be Put Into Your Living Trust

Cash. Cash cannot be put into a trust. Simply listing it will not work. You can put it in a bank account and either create a Totten trust or put the bank account into a living trust.

Retirement accounts. You should not put IRAs, 401(k)s, or profit sharing plans into a living trust, and in some cases, it is illegal to do so. Generally, you can name a beneficiary to avoid probate so there is no reason to put the accounts into a living trust.

Annuities. An annuity will generally allow you to name a beneficiary as part of the contract. The money is received by the beneficiary outside of probate.

Life insurance. When you bought the life insurance, you named the beneficiaries.

Vehicles. Some insurance companies will not insure you if the vehicle is in a trust. Most states allow a vehicle to be registered in joint tenancy to avoid probate. "Transfer-on-death" vehicle registration which avoids probate is available in California, Connecticut, Kansas, Missouri, and Ohio.

Checking account. You can put a checking account into a living trust, but if do, then the checks will name the trust as the payer.

Joint tenancy property. Property held in joint tenancy does not go through probate, so there is no need to name it in your living trust.

Community property with rights of survivorship. States that are community property states do not require shared property in the marriage to go through probate, and Alaska, Arizona, California, Nevada, Texas, and Wisconsin expressly authorize spouses to own community property in this manner.

B. People

After you have determined what property you want to include in your trust, then you need to identify who you will name as beneficiaries and who will be the trustee to manage the property in the trust. Keep in mind that many, but not all, of the laws that applied to wills are also applied to trusts.

a) Beneficiaries

A *beneficiary* is person(s) or organizations that receive the property in a trust. They do not have to be U.S. citizens or residents. When you create a trust, naming a beneficiary is required. A beneficiary's interest in a trust varies depending on the type of trust that has been created.

Property that is received by beneficiaries is not subject to Federal income tax on the amount they receive, but if the property they receives interest after they receive it, then that portion of earned interest is taxable.

Primary beneficiary. This is the person or organization who you select to be the one who gets the property when you die. You can name multiple primary beneficiaries to share property.

Alternate beneficiary. You are not required, but should name an alternate beneficiary. An alternate beneficiary gets the property should the primary beneficiary die before you or rejects the property. You can name multiple alternate beneficiaries to share the property. Naming an alternate beneficiary for the alternate beneficiary is not generally done because if both the primary beneficiary and the alternate beneficiary die, the property in the trust will go to the residuary beneficiary named in the trust.

Residuary beneficiary. A residuary beneficiary receives the property that is left in the trust that is not specifically named to a primary or alternate beneficiary.

Alternate residuary beneficiary. Just like the alternate beneficiary, the alternate residuary beneficiary is not required, but you should name one. If the residuary beneficiary dies before you or rejects the property, then the property will pass to the alternate. Naming an alternate to the alternate is not generally done.

Minor Child(ren). If you name a beneficiary who is a minor (under 18), you must name an adult to manage the property in the trust on the minor's behalf because minor cannot own property or enter into contracts. The adult who manages the property for the minor can do so until the age of 18 or until a later age which you specify in the trust.

Child(ren) born after a trust has been created. Generally, the law expects parents to provide for their child(ren) including those that are born after the creation of a legal document. Although the laws generally only name wills, courts will extend the reach to trusts if the child has not been provided for elsewhere or appropriately. The reason is that courts presume that a parent did not intentionally leave out a child simply because they were born after the date a document is entered into. To account for this in your living trust you can add a codicil.

Grandchild(ren). There is no requirement that property be left to grandchild(ren), except in certain circumstances where the parents of the grandchild(ren) have died. In which case, the grandchild(ren) take the place of the parents.

Pets. The law does not allow a pet to own property, but you can name property in a trust to someone you know will look after the pet for you. The pet will not own the property and there is likely no legal remedy if the person you name does not carry out your wishes, so choose someone you can trust.

b) Trustees

A *trustee* is a person, or organization such as a bank, who is given control or powers of administration over property in trust, with a legal obligation to administer the property solely for the purposes specified by the creator of the trust. An executor gives property to a trustee to hold for a third person. For example, an executor might give property to a trustee to care for the property of a minor child. A trustee has a role similar to the executor, but where the executor's job ends when probate ends, a trustee's job and responsibilities can continue for years, to be determined by the nature of the trust that has been created. A trust is a way to hold property, under the care of the trustee, for the benefit of another, the distribution of which will be under the discretion of the trustee, according to the rules/obligations described by the creator of the trust which, in this case, would be the testator.

Trustees have legal title of the property in a trust and are authorized to buy and sell property for the benefit of the trust without the court's, or the beneficiaries', permission. A trustee has almost absolute power over the property so it is important to put some consideration into who you name as your trustee.

The trustee must keep the beneficiaries informed about what is happening with the trust account. This notice requires enough information to determine the activities of the trust, including accounting of losses, gains, and payments made out of the trust.

The trustee is entitled to be compensated for their services. While the trustee can be paid a reasonable amount for their services, they may not make a profit at the expense of the trust. This means that the trustee cannot make a commission that would be paid by a third party. For example, if the trustee acts as a sales agent, the trustee may not earn any sales commission. If you decide to hire a trust company, such as a bank, the annual fee is usually around 1% of the trust property. Family or friends may decide not to charge you anything, or they may decide to charge you more.

Naming multiple trustees is recommended because it helps to spread around the risk of dishonest or unreliable trustees. You can name trustees as co-trustees or you can name different trustees to look after different property.

It is also recommended that you have the trustees post surety bonds, which protects the trust property. A *surety bond* is paid by the trustee in the amount that roughly equals the value of the property that is in the trust. This helps protect against fraud or reckless mismanagement by the trustee. If the trustee acts honestly, and for the benefit of the trust, then the surety bond is returned to the trustee at the completion of the trust.

IV. You Created Your Legal Document, Now What?

1. Storing Your Documents

N ow that you have created your legal documents, you need to store them. You will also need to know how to make any necessary changes. Most of the rules governing wills, also applies to trusts and powers of attorney. In this chapter, you will learn how to store and make changes to your legal documents.

A. Where to Keep It

Your legal documents should be easy for your executor and/or trustees to find and at least one other person. The people you entrust with the location of your legal documents do not need to know their contents or who you named as beneficiaries.

Generally, people store all of their legal documents together in their safety deposit box at a bank or in their house safe. These are both excellent places to store your legal documents because, if the executor or trustees do not know where your legal documents are, the safety deposit box or the house safe is a likely place they will look for the documents.

There is no legal requirement for where you should store your legal documents. That is entirely up to you.

B. How to Keep It

When you store your legal documents, you can staple the pages together along with any self-proving affidavits and/or any other documents that you want to be distributed after you die and place them in a larger envelope with "Estate Documents" written on the envelope. You may want to put your power of attorney and/or living will in a separate envelope because these documents are only effective while you are still alive.

C. Making Copies

Copying your legal documents is practical, but the copies are not legally binding without your original signatures, the signatures of your witnesses, and/or notarizations. Probate courts require originals. While the copy you make might not be legally binding, you may still want to give a copy for your executor to help them prepare for their duties.

If you make a copy of your will before it is signed, witnessed, and notarized, and *then* have all of the wills (the original and the copy) executed to be valid wills, most states allow you to have multiple, valid wills so long as they are the same. It is not advisable to do so, however, because:

- if you need to revoke your will, you will need to revoke every copy out there and they may not be easy to track down, or
- if you forget that you made duplicates and need to later revoke your will, you may have some forgotten open provisions.

- A financial durable power of attorney copy may be accepted by third parties.

2. Making Changes to Your Existing Documents

Every few years, periodically, you should review your legal documents and make any changes to reflect the property that you have acquired or changes to your life. Also, this can give you a chance to make sure that your wishes have not changed.

A. Changes in Life

You should update your legal documents following changes in your life. These events include:

- changes to your marital status such as getting married, divorced, or remarried,
- birth or adoption of children, from current or previous marriage(s), or grandchildren,
- death of a parent, spouse, child, or anyone named in your legal documents,
- significant financial losses, gains, or the addition of new debts,
- changing your state of residence, or
- buying property in another state.

B. How to Make Changes

Changes to your legal documents, made after the documents have been signed notarized and/or witnessed, can be done by including a statement that supersedes all prior documents. A statement that you put in your new legal documents that supersedes the previous one is known as a *codicil or an amendment.* Generally, it is best to add a codicil that rejects all prior documents and makes your changes in a new document.

C. Consequences of Not Making Changes

Failure to change your documents after significant life events can have unintended consequences. For example, if the people in your will are now all dead, then your will would pass according to state law, which usually means your property would pass to your relatives, and your wishes might not be fulfilled. If you have children after you create your legal documents, and no children are named in the documents because your legal documents have not been updated, then the court may end up deciding who will care for your minor children. Your estate will also have to spend the added cost of litigation for disputes of unsettled matters that are not addressed in your legal documents.

D. Revoke an Existing Legal Document

For a will, in addition to being revocable by codicil or, in special cases, by holographic will, you can also revoke the will be physical action. Physical action means tearing, burning, or, in some other way, physically destroying the will. Simply scratching out the names on your will is generally not enough.

Physically destroying any of the other legal documents will have no effect on their legality. To revoke these other legal documents, you will need to enter into a separate codicil that revokes the documents.

E. Reviving a Revoked Legal Document

When you destroy a second will by a physical action that had previously revoked a first will, the first will is not revived by your physical destruction of your second will. It is bad practice to try to do so. You can, however, create a third will that contains the same, or similar, information.

For any legal document that you revoke by codicil, no prior versions of the legal document are revived automatically. To revive an earlier version, you would need to create a third document that contains your needs.

F. If a Legal Document Is Missing At Death

If your will cannot be found at the time you die, the probate court will assume that the will has been revoked. Also, if there is a valid first will that was revoked by the missing second will, then the first will is legally valid because, remember, a will is not binding until it has been approved by a probate court. Therefore, all previous wills, that are revoked, should be physically destroyed to avoid this kind of problem and confusion.

For a living trust, you are allowed to have more than one valid living trust. If trust documents are missing, evidence can be provided of the trust's existence.

For all other documents, if the documents cannot be found when they are needed and/or at your death, then that signals to the court or third parties that the documents have been revoked.

V. Additional Resources

1. Attorney

While you are creating your legal documents, or even after you have created them, you may need additional resource. In this chapter, you will learn about retaining an attorney.

A. Hiring an Attorney

If you think you can simply complete the sample forms from a legal self-help book and have an attorney look them over for you, you may have a hard time finding an attorney that will take on the job. Even if you do find an attorney willing to take it on, you may find it to be more costly than having them create the documents. One reason may be the attorney is not completely comfortable with taking on someone's work on their reputation. If you decide to hire an attorney, there are some things to consider including the type of attorney, finding an attorney, and fees.

B. Type of an Attorney to Hire

The type of attorney that you hire depends on what problem you need to solve. For estate planning you may need an attorney who specializes in estates as well as elder, tax, real estate, or business law. Your attorney, at a minimum, should be a member of your state's bar. Because the information that you provide is very personal, you should seek an attorney that you feel comfortable talking with.

C.   Finding an Attorney

There are many ways to go about finding a competent attorney. You can ask family, friends, or businesses that you respect for recommendations. Generally, you can go to an attorney that you have been referred to even if they do not practice in estate planning. They may take you as a client, or they may refer you to someone who can. You can search online on an established online directory that allows you to narrow your search by location and practice area. However, these directories tend to list established attorneys with high fees. If you are part of a group legal plan as part of a union, employer, or consumer group, you might start with them and get your problems taken care of for free or at a reduced rate.

D.   Attorney Fees

Attorneys can be expensive. Fees commonly range from $150 to $500 per hour, or more. But, the high cost does not always translate into better service. You are better off with an attorney that understands your unique situation. Fees should be disclosed upfront and you should make sure to get something affirmative in writing. If you agree to a set price for the work to be completed, you should know what the conditions are which can change that contract price or other terms.

2. Legal Research

D oing your own legal research is a challenge because you may not know where to even go to look for resources. Even where you find information you may not know if the information you are finding is correct or up to date. For these reasons, and more, we do not recommend that you rely solely on your own legal research.

A. Law Libraries

Going to a law library and searching online can serve as a useful starting point. Most law school libraries are Federal repositories and therefore are open to the public during normal business hours. While at the law library, librarians are usually happy to help you find information and provide you with some guidance about where to begin your research. Some public libraries have some legal books that may be useful. Also, your local county courthouse may have a law library, however, selections vary.

B. Online

It is possible to find quality information online. You personally have to gauge, not only the reputation of the information that you are being presented, but also the date of the information. If you go to a law library, a librarian may recommend some online tools as well as some printed materials.

Appendix

State Specific Information

Alabama:
PeerlessLegal.com/wtpo/al-alabama/
Alaska:
PeerlessLegal.com/wtpo/ak-alaska/
Arizona:
PeerlessLegal.com/wtpo/az-arizona/
Arkansas:
PeerlessLegal.com/wtpo/ar-arkansas/
California:
PeerlessLegal.com/wtpo/ca-california/
Colorado:
PeerlessLegal.com/wtpo/co-colorado/
Connecticut:
PeerlessLegal.com/wtpo/ct-connecticut/
Delaware:
PeerlessLegal.com/wtpo/de-delaware/
District of Columbia, Washington:
PeerlessLegal.com/wtpo/dc-washington/
Florida:
PeerlessLegal.com/wtpo/fl-florida/
Georgia:
PeerlessLegal.com/wtpo/ga-georgia/
Hawaii:
PeerlessLegal.com/wtpo/hi-hawaii/
Idaho:
PeerlessLegal.com/wtpo/id-idaho/
Illinois:
PeerlessLegal.com/wtpo/il-illinois/
Indiana:
PeerlessLegal.com/wtpo/in-indiana/
Iowa:
PeerlessLegal.com/wtpo/ia-iowa/
Kansas:
PeerlessLegal.com/wtpo/ks-kansas/

Kentucky:
PeerlessLegal.com/wtpo/ky-kentucky/
Louisiana:
PeerlessLegal.com/wtpo/la-louisiana/
Maine:
PeerlessLegal.com/wtpo/me-maine/
Maryland:
PeerlessLegal.com/wtpo/md-maryland/
Massachusetts:
PeerlessLegal.com/wtpo/ma-massachusetts/
Michigan:
PeerlessLegal.com/wtpo/mi-michigan/
Minnesota:
PeerlessLegal.com/wtpo/mn-minnesota/
Mississippi:
PeerlessLegal.com/wtpo/ms-mississippi/
Missouri:
PeerlessLegal.com/wtpo/mo-missouri/
Montana:
PeerlessLegal.com/wtpo/mt-montana/
Nebraska:
PeerlessLegal.com/wtpo/ne-nebraska/
Nevada:
PeerlessLegal.com/wtpo/nv-nevada/
New Hampshire:
PeerlessLegal.com/wtpo/nh-new-hampshire/
New Jersey:
PeerlessLegal.com/wtpo/nj-new-jersey/
New Mexico:
PeerlessLegal.com/wtpo/nm-new-mexico/
New York:
PeerlessLegal.com/wtpo/ny-new-york/
North Carolina:
PeerlessLegal.com/wtpo/nc-north-carolina/
North Dakota:
PeerlessLegal.com/wtpo/nd-north-dakota/

Ohio:
PeerlessLegal.com/wtpo/oh-ohio/
Oklahoma:
PeerlessLegal.com/wtpo/ok-oklahoma/
Oregon:
PeerlessLegal.com/wtpo/or-oregon/
Pennsylvania:
PeerlessLegal.com/wtpo/pa-pennsylvania/
Rhode Island:
PeerlessLegal.com/wtpo/ri-rhode-island/
South Carolina:
PeerlessLegal.com/wtpo/sc-south-carolina/
South Dakota:
PeerlessLegal.com/wtpo/sd-south-dakota/
Tennessee:
PeerlessLegal.com/wtpo/tn-tennessee/
Texas:
PeerlessLegal.com/wtpo/tx-texas/
Utah:
PeerlessLegal.com/wtpo/ut-utah/
Vermont:
PeerlessLegal.com/wtpo/vt-vermont/
Virginia:
PeerlessLegal.com/wtpo/va-virginia/
Washington (State):
PeerlessLegal.com/wtpo/wa-washington/
West Virginia:
PeerlessLegal.com/wtpo/wv-west-virginia/
Wisconsin:
PeerlessLegal.com/wtpo/wi-wisconsin/
Wyoming:
PeerlessLegal.com/wtpo/wy-wyoming/

Glossary

AB Trust. Spousal tax saving estate trust where the surviving spouse leaves property in "Trust A" and allows the spouse use of the property during the spouse's lifetime, and authorizes limited rights to invade the trust principal. After the surviving spouse's death, the trust property goes to the beneficiaries.

AB Disclaimer Trust. Similar to an AB Trust, the surviving spouse decides how much, if any, of deceased spouse property will be places in Trust A.

Acknowledgement. A statement in front of a person qualified to administer an oath (notary public) that a document with a person's signature was actually signed by the person claimed on the document.

Administration of an Estate. A court supervised distribution of the probate estate of decedent. The manager of the distribution is the executor if there is a will, and if there is not will, then this person is called an administrator. In a few states the personal representative takes either one of these roles.

Administrator. Someone not named in the decedent's will and acts as a personal representative.

Adult. Generally, someone that is over the age of 18.

Affidavit. A written statement that is signed under oath in front of a notary public.

Alternate Beneficiary. If a primary beneficiary dies before the person who creates the will or trust does, then the property will pass to the alternate beneficiary.

Augmented Estate. Property left by will plus certain property transferred outside of the will by gifts, joint tenancies, and living trusts. Augmented estates are calculated if a surviving spouse wants to claim their statutory share of the deceased spouse's property. A surviving spouse is considered to be adequately provided for it they receive at least one-third of the augmented estate.

Basis. A tax term dealing with valuation of property for determining profit or loss on sale. Example, if you buy a house for $100,000, then your basis will be $100,000. If you sell your house for $150,000, then your taxable profit will be $50,000.

Beneficiary. The named recipient of an asset belonging to a decedent in a will or trust.

Bequest. A gift that becomes effective at the time of death.

Bond. Monetary guarantees that an estate, a trust, or a custodianship from the dishonest acts of a fiduciary.

Bypass Trust. Also called an AB Trust.

Certification. In the presence of a notary public who acknowledges you signing and dating a living trust.

Child's Trust. A trust created for a young beneficiary that has not reached the age specified by the grantor (can be greater than 18 years of age) or age 35, whichever comes first.

Codicil. An amendment to a will.

Common Law Marriage. Only in a handful of states, a common law marriage is where the state recognizes a couple as being married if they have lived together for a certain amount of time and intent to be husband and wife.

Community Property. Any and all property acquired during a marriage from the efforts of one or both of the spouses. Only used in Arizona, California, Idaho, Louisiana, Nevada, New Mexico, Texas, Washington (State), and Wisconsin.

Conservator. Appointed by the court, it is someone who manages the affairs of a mentally incompetent person. Also called a guardian in a few states.

Creditor. Institution or person to whom money is owed.

Custodian. A person appointed under the Uniform Gift of Minors Act (also used interchangeably with the name Uniform Transfers to Minors Act), who has a fiduciary position over assets for the benefit of a minor. The custodian can use the property for the benefit of the minor child including for the minor's health, education, or other support. Court does not supervise the custodian.

Debtor. A person who owes money.

Deceased Spouse. It is the first spouse to die in a living trust or an AB Trust.

Decedent. Person who died.

Decedent's Trust. Trust created at the decedent's death to take advantage of decedent's Federal estate tax exemption.

Deed. The legal document that transfers real estate title.

Descendant. Any person born into the family line e.g., daughter, son, grandchild.

Devise. A bequest of real property and in many States is used interchangeably with bequest.

Devisee. Someone who has been left real property in a will.

Disclaimer Trust. Trust where a beneficiary has the specific right to disclaim all or any part of a gift left them in the trust, and the gift will then pass to the next in line.

Disinheritance Clause. Clause stating that all persons other than your specifically named beneficiaries are disinherited.

Domicile. The state or country of primary residence.

Donee. Someone who receives a gift.

Donor. Someone who gives a gift.

Durable Power of Attorney. A power of attorney that survives the maker's (principal) incapacity.

Estate. Generally referred to as all of the property you own on your death.

Executor. A person named in the decedent's will who will manage the decedent's estate including having the estate go through probate court, collect the assets, and distribute them. Some states call the executor the personal representative.

Execution. The act of signing a will by the testator and the witnesses.

Fiduciary. The duty to act on someone else's behalf in a fair and trustworthy manner. The person who holds this duty is also called a fiduciary.

Gift. Property given to another person or organization. This can happen after or before death, or using a will or trust.

Grantor. Same as settlor. The person who creates a trust.

Guardian. Appointed person to look after a minor and/or the minor's estate.

Heir. Entitlement of an asset of a decedent when no person is named as the beneficiary of that asset.

Holographic Will. A handwritten will by the testator of the essential terms. To be legal, the holographic will requires the testator's signature anywhere on the will (signature does not necessarily have to be at the end of the holographic will), and does not require witnesses. Not valid in all states.

Inherit. Receiving property upon the death of another.

Instrument. Legal jargon often used to refer to a document.

Inter Vivos Trust. Also called a living trust. A trust created during a lifetime (versus one created at the time of death). Generally, the trust is for the benefit of the person creating the trust, but is irrevocable on death of the creator.

Intestate. Someone who dies with no will.

Intestate Succession. Decedent's property is distributed to the decedent's heirs when there is no will or the will fails to distribute the decedent's property.

Irrevocable Trust. A trust that once created cannot be revoked or amended by the person who created it.

Issue. The lineal descendants of a person e.g., your children, grandchildren.

Joint Tenancy. Written title naming one or more persons as equal owners (called joint tenants), and upon the death of a joint tenant, the remaining joint tenants take the share of the decreased joint tenancy by right of survivorship, regardless of contrary provisions in a will. Joint tenancy is not favored by courts so creation of joint tenancy generally requires exact language. Example: A, B, and C are joint tenants in Greenacre.

A dies. B and C are joint tenant is Greenacre and the heirs of A have no interest in Greenacre. The last one to outlive between B and C takes all of Greenacre.

Legacy. Gift given of personal property in a will.

Life Estate. Right given to use of property for the life a person. No right of transfer or interest is given to the property. At the death of the measuring life, the life estate ends and all interests are retained by the grantor.

Living Trust. Also called an inter vivos trust. Trust created during the life of a person, and is generally for the benefit of the person who creates the trust, but it becomes irrevocable upon the death of the person who creates the trust.

Living Will. A document that tells doctors and other healthcare professionals whether you want to have your life prolonged through artificial means such as a respirator.

Marital Property. Property acquired during a marriage from the efforts of one or more of the spouses.

Marital Trust. Trust created at death, and for the benefit off the decedent spouse to take advantage of Federal estate tax exemptions. The surviving spouse is not able to make changes to the trust.

Minor. Someone under the age of majority, generally 18 years of age.

Mortgage. A document that has a real estate as its collateral until the payment of debt is complete.

Notary Public. A person authorized by a state to administer oaths.

Payable on Death (POD). An account (often a bank account) that will pass to a designated beneficiary on the owner's death.

Personal Guardian. An adult appointed or selected to care for a minor child in the event no biological or adoptive parents take responsibility for the child.

Personal Property. Everything else that is not real estate. This would include vehicles, cash, and pets.

Pour-Over Will. Property left through the will must go through probate before it goes into the trust i.e., a will that "pours over" property into a trust.

Power of Attorney. An authorization of someone other than you to act on your behalf.

Primary Beneficiary. The person who directly inherits property in a will or trust, but does not have rights of ownership until after the death of the creator of the will or trust.

Principal. Property owned by a trust. Also used to refer to income generated by a property.

Probate Code. Statutes in almost every state that govern wills, trusts, and probate.

Probate Court. Supervised changes of titles of assets from a decedent's name to the name of the beneficiaries under the decedent's will or decedent's heirs if the decedent died without a will.

Probate Estate. All of decedent's property that passes through probate i.e., all property owned at death that is not held in joint tenancy, a living trust, a bank account trust, or in a life insurance policy.

Property Guardian. Person named in a will to take care of property given to a minor child.

Quasi-Community Property. Property that is acquired in a state that is not a community property, during a marriage, and dies in a community property state with the property being physically in the community property state; the property is treated as community property.

Real Property. Land, buildings on land, long-term leases, rights to minerals, condominiums, and co-ops. Also called real estate.

Recording. Filing a copy of a deed with the county land records office that the land sits on. This is considered a public record.

Remainder. The balances on the estate after all of the specific gifts have been distributed.

Remainderman. The person who will take the property after the life usage of the property by another e.g., if the testator bequeaths a life estate in testator's residence to A, and then at A's death, the residence will pass to B; B would be the remainderman.

Residuary Beneficiary. The beneficiary receives any property that the will creator owned at the time of death but did not leave to beneficiaries by will or otherwise.

Residue. Assets in an estate or will that are left over after distribution of all of the specific bequests.

Restatement. Restating terms of the living trust and acts as an amendment and a way of revoking the living trust.

Self-Proving Affidavit. Legal in most state, it is a document stating a witness will not be required to testify in court to prove a will offered for probate is the last will of testament of the decedent.

Self-Proving Will. Where a will is self-proving under the law of a state, then nearly all states will allow the will's admission into probate of uncontested wills without testimony of a witness to the will. In California, a will is self-proving if the witnesses attest, under penalty and perjury, that the will was property executed.

Separate Property. Property belonging entirely to one person.

Settlor. The one who creates the trust.

Successor Trustee. Person or entity (e.g., business) who serves a trustee of a trust document on the resignation, removal, or death of a trustee. For most living trusts, this is the person or entity named to act as trustee once the original trustee is no longer able to serve as trustee.

Surety Bond. A type of inexpensive insurance to guarantee the executor will act honestly; the bond is posted by the executor in an equal amount to the value of personal property in the estate (not allowed for real estate).

Survivor's Trust. Trust created after the death for the benefit of decedent's spouse to take advantage of Federal estate tax exemptions, and the surviving spouse has the power to make changes the trust.

Tenancy by the entirety. Property that is owned by married people in a state that recognizes tenancy by the entirety. The property owned and acquired during the marriage will be held as joint tenants.

Tenancy in Common. Ownership of property between two or more people to own property as co-owners but with each retaining their complete interest, including the right to leave their share of their property to their heirs.

Testate. When a person dies with no will.

Testator. The one whose will is being discussed.

Title. A document proving ownership of property.

Totten Trust. Designated assets as "in trust for" another.

Transfer on Death (TOD). Account that passes directly to a designated beneficiary on the owner's death.

Trust. Legal entity and relationship where one person or entity holds legal title and responsibility to property for the financial benefit of another person or entity.

Trustee. Person holding title to trust assets for the benefit of the beneficiary of the trust, and is responsible for management of trust assets and has a fiduciary relationship to the beneficiaries of the trust.

Uniform Gift of Minors Act. A statute adopted by most states that provides a method for transferring property to minors and arranging for an adult to manage it until the child is no longer a child (usually 18). Also goes by the name Uniform Transfers to Minors Act (UTMA).

Will. A written document created at the death of someone to direct distribution of their assets. A will is generally not going to affect assets held in joint tenancy, distributed in a contract (e.g., life insurance policy, pension, annuity.), or property subject to a payable on death or transfer on death designation.

Witnesses. Person who sees a testator sign their will and signs the will after the testator. The witness generally must be at least 18 years of age, know that the document being signed is a will, and is not entitled to anything in the will.

Index

A

B

C

D

E

F

G

H

I

J

Bestselling titles:

Will, Trust, & Power of Attorney Creator and Estate Records Organizer: Legal Self-Help Guide

Guidance On Creating Your Own Will & Power of Attorney: Legal Self-Help Guide

Simple Will Creator: Legal Self-Help Guide

Give Through A Will & Living Trust: Legal Self-Help Guide

8 Living Trust Forms: Legal Self-Help Guide

Made in the USA
Monee, IL
13 June 2022

97968429R00095